Praise for *Demand the Impossible!*

"For Bill Ayers, it is the freedom of our collective imagination that links the contemporary world—ensconced as it is in pervasive militarism, racist violence, and environmental devastation—to the flourishing of our planet. This is a manifesto that should be read by everyone who wants to believe that 'another world is possible.'"

—Angela Y. Davis, author of *Abolition Democracy: Beyond Empire, Prisons, and Torture* and *Freedom Is a Constant Struggle: Ferguson, Palestine, and the Foundations of a Movement*

"With huge numbers of us recognizing the need for transformative change, this ambitious and exuberant book perfectly matches its historical moment. Ayers fearlessly confronts the intersecting crises of our age—endless war, surging inequality, unchecked white supremacy and perilous planetary warming—while mapping emancipatory new possibilities. From the first page, his courage is contagious."

—Naomi Klein, author of *This Changes Everything* and *The Shock Doctrine: The Rise of Disaster Capitalism*

"*Demand the Impossible!* is more than a book, more than a manifesto. It is a torch. Bill Ayers's vision for a humane future is incendiary—fire that incinerates old logics and illuminates new paths. If we do not end the violence of militarism, materialism, caging, dispossession, debt, want, ignorance, and global warming, our very survival is impossible. Read aloud."

—Robin D. G. Kelley, author of *Freedom Dreams: The Black Radical Imagination*

"With the beautiful idealism of a young radical and the sage wisdom of an elder, Bill Ayers is making trouble again, and we should all be grateful. In *Demand the Impossible!* Ayers troubles the waters of staid political practices, insisting that we close our eyes for a moment and think creatively about what a better world might look like, and then open our eyes wide and organize boldly to make that world a reality. This is an elegant and provocative manifesto for our time, one that honors the social justice organizing currently in motion."

—Barbara Ransby, author of *Ella Baker and the Black Freedom Movement*

"Bill Ayers has produced a portrait of two worlds. One is a dystopia, recognizable as the world in which we live, the other a world that capitalism describes as a fantasy—a world reconstructed around values that place the advancement of humanity and the sanctity of the planet above the accumulation of wealth and power. The two portraits stand in dramatic contrast and make *Demand the Impossible!* both illuminating and compelling. This manifesto is radical less in its rhetoric than in its daring to actually go to the roots of the barbarism of the capitalist system. *Demand the Impossible!* is to be read and then shared widely. It can serve as a motivator for those of us engaged in the long battle for justice and social transformation."

—Bill Fletcher, Jr., coauthor of *Solidarity Divided: The Crisis in Organized Labor and a New Path toward Social Justice*

"In his many years of practicing and theorizing pedagogy, Bill Ayers has proven himself a master teacher. Now, *Demand the Impossible!* is a brilliant and accessible distillation of techniques and knowledge crafted into a powerful manifesto for our times, expanding the horizon of our expectations."

—Roxanne Dunbar-Ortiz, author of *An Indigenous Peoples' History of the United States*

"Bill Ayers is the philosopher of the revolutionary spirit. These are despondent times, and yet, as Bill muses—history can surprise us. In preparation for that surprise, Bill has written a smart and inspirational manifesto."

—Vijay Prashad, author of *The Poorer Nations: A Possible History of the Global South*

"Bill Ayers's *Demand the Impossible!* is a strong shot of inspiration for anyone searching for deep social transformation. It is a heartfelt, upbeat manifesto in favor of activism as an antidote to despair. Chockfull of personal stories, real facts, and concrete examples packaged in exquisite writing, *Demand the Impossible!* will open your mind to possibilities you never thought existed. Ayers will get you off your seat and into the street, fist raised, heart full, reaching for the spectacular."

—Medea Benjamin, cofounder of Code Pink and author of *Drone Warfare: Killing by Remote Control*

"*Demand the Impossible!* is a timely call to action, a manifesto that lays out the challenges we currently face and pushes us to imagine a more just and peaceful world. 'What if we resisted the logics of war? What if we embraced the idea of abolishing the prison industrial complex? What if we followed the lead of the courageous young people currently challenging police power? What if we took seriously that another world is possible?' Bill Ayers writes clearly and passionately about these and other important issues like economic and environmental justice. Read *Demand the Impossible!* to unleash your radical imagination and to gain insight into how we can and must transform society."

—Mariame Kaba, founder/director of Project NIA

"*Demand the Impossible!* is just what the world needs right now, a manifesto that challenges us to imagine bigger, love harder, create more expansively, and struggle toward a liberatory future in spite of our deepest doubts. Bill Ayers wakes us up and shows us that even the most entrenched, most permanent-seeming institutions—the military, the prison, the police, capitalism itself—are no match for the creativity and determination of the 'universal family' and the 'better angels of ourselves.' *Demand the Impossible!* is a call to abandon the illusory American Dream wholesale, and, in its place, to unleash our own collective, revolutionary dreams into the universe. I dare you to not be inspired by this book."

—Maya Schenwar, editor of *Truthout* and
author of *Locked Down, Locked Out*

"Bill Ayers reminds us that radical social change, including revolution, is begun and sustained not by the practical, but by those possessed by a messianic vision, one that is worth fighting and even dying to achieve. Without this vision, and the steadfastness required to sustain it, nothing important is accomplished. We live in a moment in human history when only those who dare to defy all odds, only those who resist, not because they will win but because it is right, will make change possible."

—Chris Hedges, author of *War Is a Force That
Gives Us Meaning* and *Wages of Rebellion*

"This is a deeply refreshing book, reminding us that the core principles of socialist and anarchist thought—peace, justice, freedom, equality—are grounded not in utopian fantasy but in the joyous work of the creative imagination in everyday life. In large ways (an end to the military-industrial complex and the US prison system) and small (the rebirth of community and public life in neighborhoods) Ayers offers a program that is long on ideals and even longer on actually existing programs, groups, movements, and individuals working toward a humane future. By turns alarming in its realistic assessment of the madness and stupidity of the present global system and inspiring in its down-to-earth proposals for alternative human futures, this is a must-read for discouraged progressives everywhere. It is a book that could be a clear and present danger to Western civilization as we know it—and in the very best way."

—W. J. T. Mitchell, editor of *Critical Inquiry* and author
of *Seeing through Race* and *Cloning Terror*

"Every once in a while a book comes along that not only changes the way one thinks, but opens a new space for imagining and then acting to create a better world with commitment, courage, and a heightened sense of ethical and social responsibility. *Demand the Impossible!* is one of those books, and it ranks right at the top of the list. Ayers has a gift—he not only writes like a poet but he never fails to deal with rigorous and important ideas in an accessible and moving style. Touching on a range of issues extending from police violence and racism to ecological destruction, Ayers raises all the right questions and connects the dots that provide a tapestry for energizing the radical imagination. This may be one of the best books written in that tradition. Powerful, insightful, prodding, challenging, and most of all hopeful—if you want to understand the problems facing a society tipping into the abyss of authoritarianism, this book is a must-read, a kind of master text for those of us figuring out how to change a world that seems at times beyond our reach."

—Henry Giroux, author of *Theory and Resistance in Education* and *The Violence of Organized Forgetting*

"*Demand the Impossible!* provides the imperative we need now. As public consciousness and despair heighten in our various locales, we must be willing to engage lessons from the past and present while building a future that is reflective of our commitment to justice. If we're serious about this, we know there is no choice: all we got is US!"

—David Stovall, author of *Born Out of Struggle*

✳ ✳ ✳

DEMAND
THE
IMPOSSIBLE!

A Radical Manifesto

BILL AYERS

Haymarket Books
Chicago, Illinois

Published in 2016 by
Haymarket Books
P.O. Box 180165
Chicago, IL 60618
773-583-7884
www.haymarketbooks.org
info@haymarketbooks.org

ISBN: 978-1-60846-670-2

Trade distribution:
In the US, Consortium Book Sales and Distribution, www.cbsd.com
In Canada, Publishers Group Canada, www.pgcbooks.ca
In the UK, Turnaround Publisher Services, www.turnaround-uk.com
All other countries, Publishers Group Worldwide, www.pgw.com

This book was published with the generous support of Wallace
Action Fund and Lannan Foundation.

Cover design by Rachel Cohen.
Interior art by Nathaly Bonilla, nathalybonilla.tumblr.com.

Printed in Canada by union labor.

Library of Congress Cataloging-in-Publication data is available.

10 9 8 7 6 5 4 3 2 1

Be realistic, demand the impossible!

—Che Guevara

For the extraordinary James Thindwa, who challenges and inspires me day in and day out with his ability to make a concrete analysis of real conditions, and then to do the work that needs to be done—again and again. And for all the other beautiful people rising up against the odds for justice—for a world where no one is so wealthy that they can buy another human being, and none so needy that they must sell themselves in order to survive—and for all those who will join us by and by

CONTENTS

The smart way to keep people passive and obedient is to strictly limit the spectrum of acceptable opinion, but allow very lively debate within that spectrum— even encourage the more critical and dissident views. That gives people the sense that there's free thinking going on, while all the time the presuppositions of the system are being reinforced by the limits put on the range of the debate.

—Noam Chomsky

*In a room where
people unanimously maintain
a conspiracy of silence,
one word of truth
sounds like a pistol shot.*

—Czesław Miłosz

I was invited to give a talk at an "international anarchist convention" in Greece in 2011, and while I had a lovely correspondence with the rebels who'd organized the event, and they'd assured me that they would cover my airfare and put me up for a few days at one of their squats, I was skeptical—they were anarchists after all. But once I'd cleared customs and two skinny kids—frighteningly pierced and wildly tattooed, neon-colored hair flying haphazardly from their skulls—rushed me wearing vibrant rags and big welcoming smiles, I thought, *Whatever*. I was happy to be there.

We jumped on a bus and headed for one of the dicey districts of Athens, and they broke out a thermos of thick black coffee and a bag of Arab food, grease darkening the paper sack in a delicate Rorschach, and we dived eagerly in. They offered portions to our dubious fellow travelers—"We're anarchists!" they proclaimed—and we chattered happily about plans for the week as they pointed out the ancient sights along the way.

"An anarchist convention," I said, as we rolled through the city streets. "Isn't that a contradiction in terms, like jumbo shrimp or Justice Roberts?" And a keynote speech seemed so unnecessarily hierarchical. "Are you sure you're anarchists?" I teased. "Don't be fooled," one of them kidded back. "This is all a front for chaos and confusion. You're one of our many props!"

The squat was beautiful—open windows and unlocked doors, assorted chairs in all manner of disrepair in the large commons area, pirated electricity and Internet, big pots of black beans and lentils bubbling away on a small black stove, and a huge salvaged wooden table overflowing with black bread, apples and cheese, olives, tomatoes, and hard-boiled eggs. Later that night I spoke to a large gathering at an arts college about our shared values of peace and popular justice, human agency and mass mobilization from below, and the importance of refusing to bow down to either gods or masters. I noted Mikhail Bakunin's insight that freedom without socialism is a license for privilege and injustice, while socialism without freedom can become slavery and brutality, and I ended by saluting the great participatory tradition in Greece stretching back centuries and sustained by subsequent generations of Greek youth. Carry it on!

All of this was prelude to an encounter that is as vivid for me today as the moment it occurred, a story I've retold and re-lived many times since. Early the next morning I caught the fast boat from Piraeus to the faraway island of Paros where I was to spend the day with the legendary Manolis Glezos. We were introduced by mutual friends, and while you may not recognize the name, Manolis was the most respected (or reviled) man in all of Greece, and well known throughout Europe for a dazzling illegal act he committed in 1941. When he was still a teenager, Manolis had climbed the Acropolis with a friend and torn down and destroyed the Nazi flag that had flown over Athens since German occupation forces marched into the city a month earlier. This symbolic action (an act of terror according to the fascists) was magnified many times when the Nazis, determined to nip all opposition in the bud lest the virus of resistance spread, sentenced Manolis to death in absentia. When he was captured several months later, he was thrown into prison and tortured.

Manolis was ninety years old when we met up, a veteran of over seventy years of struggle for peace and justice — he'd been imprisoned by the German occupiers, the Italians, the Greek collaborators, and the Regime of the Colonels, adding up to more than a decade behind bars. He had been sentenced to death multiple times, charged with espionage, treason, and sabotage, and escaped prison more than once. He'd been the focus of widespread international protests and "Free Glezos!" campaigns on several occasions over the years, which surely explained why Manolis was still alive and standing at the dock waving happily when I arrived.

His broad smile emerged from his bushy white mustache and drove a deeper crease across his already-wrinkled face. He was wearing a loosely fitted coarse cotton shirt with pants to match, a beige scarf, and a light sports coat buttoned to the top. We embraced for a long moment, then turned and walked arm in arm to a café in the plaza.

Our walk was slow, for every person we passed—every one, no exception—greeted Manolis and presented a kiss or a handshake or a hug, and he offered an embrace or a word to each in return; it became the customary practice of our day together, and I assumed of his life all the time: he was a flesh-and-blood human being, to be sure, but he was simultaneously larger than life, a symbol and an icon. He bore the responsibility gracefully without being in its thrall, responding warmly to everyone he met but remaining as ordinary and earthbound and humble as anyone I've known.

I asked him about his time in the Greek Parliament and he said that each time he ran and particularly when he was elected it was always as part of a larger strategy, a useful tactic for him and his comrades at specific times but never an end in itself. "I'm interested in people collectively discovering their own power," he said. "That's an entirely different thing from an individual or a party in power."

Manolis told me about the years when he was the elected president of the Community Council in Aperathu, an experiment in far-reaching participatory democracy. "We governed by consensus," he said, "in a local assembly with forums reminiscent of the period of radical democracy in ancient Greece." They abolished all privileges for elected officials, developed a written constitution, and challenged the idea that "experts" or professional politicians and self-proclaimed leaders were better at running the town's affairs than ordinary people. "Every cook can govern!" was a kind of theme and watchword.

Manolis put his face close to mine and said with conspiratorial conviction, "The biggest obstacle to revolution here—and I'll bet it's true in your country as well—is a serious and often unrecognized lack of confidence." I thought he made sense. "We spend our lives in the presence of mayors and governors and presidents and chiefs of police," Manolis continued, "and then we lose our power of self-reliance, and we doubt that we could live without those authorities. We worship them in spite of ourselves, we may not mean to but we do, and soon enough we embrace our own passivity and become enslaved to a culture of obedience. That's a core of our weakness. That's something you and I must challenge and change." We must unleash our most radical imaginations and push ourselves to break the straitjackets of conventional thinking. Yes! We must demand the impossible.

Manolis has been arrested by riot police in front of the Parliament building each year since our meeting, still living the activist life, still battling the murderous system of oppression and exploitation, still opening spaces for more participatory democracy, more peace, and more justice. I can see him in my mind's eye now, waving cheerfully from the dock as I left later in the day—filled with energy and hope. Still demanding the impossible.

What if? That humble question might be the single spark that can ignite a massive prairie fire, provoking us to leap beyond personal speculation and into the vortex of political struggle and social action. *This is how it's always been; this is the world as we've always known it.* But why is it so? Who benefits and

who suffers? How did we get here and where do we want to
go? What if we took a radically different angle of regard and
questioned the insistent dogma of common sense? What if
we unleashed our wildest imaginations? The "what if" question might then blow open the spectrum of acceptable possibilities and take us down a rabbit hole or up into orbit—onto
one of life's restless and relentless journeys, exploring and ex-
perimenting, orbiting and spinning, inventing and adapting,
struggling toward knowledge and enlightenment, freedom
and liberation, fighting to know more in order to do more.

What if? Copernicus and Galileo challenged the dogma
of their day as they reimagined the movements of the heav-
enly bodies and the revolutions of the sun and the Earth.
Virginia Woolf breathed in a revolutionary wave of women's
freedom and imagined a room of her own, signaling in lyrical
words that everything henceforth would be new, and everything old immediately put on trial. John Coltrane heard free
jazz—devout and large—inside his head before it burst like a
shot through his horn and into our collective consciousness,
and Lin-Manuel Miranda upended the Broadway stage as he
reimagined the Founding Fathers as young Black and Latino
revolutionaries, casting a bright light on the nation's begin-
nings as well as a new perspective on contemporary struggles
for self-determination and freedom. Each of these propulsive
pioneers questioned the expected, changed the frame, and
opened a space of possibility; each rose up in the company of
others; each began with a revolutionary's dream that pushed
beyond the obvious and the settled, and evoked an alternative
universe. And each reminds us that standing next to the world

as it is, the world we might mistakenly take as immutable, we can discover or search out a wider range of possible worlds, that is, alternatives that could be or should be. Our common task is to face one another authentically and without masks, to tell our complex and various stories candidly, to break the suffocating stranglehold of common sense. "What would happen if one woman told the truth about her life?" asked the poet Muriel Rukeyser. "The world would split open." This is a call to go to the root, to question and seek evidence and to find alternatives, to speak our truths and to join together in the business of splitting the world wide open once more.

When "What if?" is taken up collectively it can be forged into a powerful tool with the potential to crack open the given world and provide previously unthinkable alternatives: "What would happen if we abolished slavery?" Boom! The runaways, the abolitionists, Denmark Vesey, Frederick Douglass, John Brown, and Harriet Tubman stoked a revolution, organizing and unleashing the agency of enslaved people everywhere and challenging the slaveocracy at its base — picture General Tubman with her laser-like focus and that small, discreet pistol in her pocket, leading the troops toward freedom. "What if we took the next step in the Black freedom movement?" Dam! Ella Baker, Fannie Lou Hamer, Joanne Robinson, Septima Clark, and their comrades in the 1960s conceived of a revolution that could create — from a world of toil and trouble — a beloved community where Black people would be free and all of us could become equals before one another and the law. Today's freedom fighters dare to proclaim once more that Black Lives Matter as they open a fresh space to join the unfinished revolution right here, right now.

Here, then, is a partial diagram of the known world, a rough sketch of what is, but certainly not a picture of what could be or should be:

- ✳ An empire unapologetically resurrected in a cauldron of deliberately constructed fear, and in the name of renewed patriotic nationalism.

- ✳ Unprecedented military expansion, a state of permanent war and the creation of a war culture, a gulag that stretches the length and breadth of the country, where mass incarceration is a defining characteristic in the "land of the free," and white supremacy reigns triumphant in the "home of the brave."

- ✳ Militarized police forces acting as aggressive occupying armies in poor communities, and the never-ending serial shootings of Black citizens.

- ✳ The identification of opaque and ill-defined enemies —"illegal" immigrants, border violators, Muslims, Arabs, foreigners, queers, Black people, independent women, terrorists—as a unifying cause.

- ✳ A panopticon-like existence in which we are all aware of being under constant surveillance—cameras everywhere, mountains of data from our purchase and travel patterns to reading and information preferences accumulating in some dark basement or shiny supercomputer—but have been forbidden from watching them watching us. We're assured by the state and the media (as well as by our families and friends and neighbors on occasion) that if we aren't doing anything wrong, we have nothing to hide, and should, then, have no objection to standing naked under the bright lights and ceaseless scrutiny of the state.

* Ritual searches, ID checks, and pat downs ("Assume the position!") at airports, train stations, and athletic events, which do little or nothing to enhance safety or security but serve a serious purpose nonetheless, functioning as metaphor and theater, a reminder that we are always at war, always at risk, and always observed—the threat level for many years a never-changing if ill-defined and meaningless "orange"—and as dress rehearsal for police and military actions that can override liberties and rights without constraint or objection.

* The eclipse of the public, the frantic pace of privatization and the fire sale of the public square—the public schools and public housing, prisons and the military, and in Chicago, the bridges and parking meters—all of which represent the triumph of corporate power and a kind of fatal entangling of corporations with the state, leading to a thieves' paradise in government with the arid ideology of capital and the "market" promoted as the truest expression of authentic participatory democracy.

✳ Galloping disparities between the haves and the have-nots—the metaphoric 1 percent and everyone else—both at home and on a global scale.

✳ A steady drumbeat of "public secrets"—obvious lies issued by the powerful like, "We don't torture" or "We don't spy on Americans" or "We shot him because he was a clear threat to the officer" or "We don't bomb civilians," whose purpose is both future deniability and evidence of power's arrogant ability to have its way regardless of truth or evidence, law or popular will.

✳ Disdain for the arts, for intellectual life, for reason and evidence, and deep contempt for the necessary back and forth of serious argument or discussion in favor of a nasty dialogue of the deaf.

✳ Formation of "popular" movements in the streets, apparently spontaneous but in reality well funded and highly organized, based on bigotry, intolerance, and the threat of violence, all of it fueled by the demonization of targeted, distinct racial, religious, or gendered vulnerable populations and the creation of convenient sacrificial scapegoats.

✳ Cataclysmic human-made climate change—hurricanes, melting ice caps, raging wildfires and deforestation, rising oceans, the shredding of the Earth's protective shield, and more—driven by unchecked extraction, reckless acquisitiveness, and the everyday operations of predatory capitalism.

Countless contradictions abound: appalling poverty and unprecedented wealth, acts of war and words of peace, liveliness and chronic social depression, hope and despair. Reality TV and then reality itself. It's a land of wild diversity, extremes and opposites, conflict and contestation, moments of personal joy, happiness, and ecstasy against times of collective rage and anguish.

Still, the bullet points above—and I use the term deliberately—are pistol shots that represent a bright thread that is recognizable and knowable. The US juggernaut is headed for catastrophe, either a new and sophisticated—dare we say it?—form of friendly looking and familiar fascism, or some other form of extreme social disintegration. Another world is surely coming—greater equality, socialism, participatory democracy, and peace are all within our reach, but nuclear war, work camps, and slavery are also possibilities. There are still choices and options, and nothing is guaranteed. Where do we go from here? A season of light or a season of darkness? Chaos or community? Barbarism or socialism?

What if we initiated a bold truth-and-reconciliation process that reached back to the start—to the theft of Native lands and the mass destruction of First Nations peoples, to the horrors and the continuing afterlife of slavery, to the accumulation of wealth based on conquest and exploitation—and faced reality in the interest of repairing historical wrongs?

What if we broke from the dogma of militarism—rejecting the anemic and seemingly endless debates about whether the United States should bomb this country or instead boycott some other country on the State Department's or Pentagon's list of targets—and organized an irresistible social upheaval strong enough to stop US invasions and conquest. What if we occupied bases, blocked munitions shipments and private militias, boycotted arms dealers, sabotaged surveillance operations and drone manufacturers—and forced the US government to disarm and close all foreign military bases within a year? Is that unthinkable? Why? Or what if we built a colossal transnational movement that organized shadow elections (initially), inviting any resident of a country with a US military presence within its borders to vote in US national elections?

What if we stopped tinkering with the business of caging people and abolished the prisons altogether? Seriously. What else would have to change to make prison abolition conceivable? And why is it easier to imagine the end of the world (in movies and comics and novels) than it is to imagine the end of prisons? Or the end of capitalism?

What if we converted the American financial industry into a public utility, community owned and popularly managed? What if we demilitarized and disarmed the police forces and reorganized them under elected and transparent community boards? What if we linked arms with National Nurses United and allied health workers, took over hospitals and clinics, and barricaded the insurance and pharmaceutical profiteers in their offices as we built a powerful popular movement to create free universal health care for all? What if teachers, students, parents, families, and community members built one big union and seized the public schools in order to teach freedom, directing our efforts to the full development of each and all? What if we organized ourselves to create free, public neighborhood/community schools designed for the many, not the few—the privileged or the lucky or the elite—and took as a reasonable standard of support the generous average cost it took to educate the children of the last five US presidents? What if we successfully blockaded every fossil fuel drilling and fracking site? Or what if we took control of the top five energy corporations and placed them under popular control?

Questions like these might inspire quixotic daydreaming or curious conjecture, but what if instead they stirred us to create alternatives, to reach for the spectacular, and to get busy with projects of reframing and repair, movement-making, agitating, educating, community organizing, and action. Plunging into the debris we see all around us, swimming as hard as we're able toward a distant and indistinct shore with courage and hope and love, overcoming difficulties and reimagining life's possibilities along the way—this is the spirit these questions might unleash in each and all of us. The questions then grow into calls to action: Disarm! Abolish the prisons! Seize big pharma and big oil! Stop the cops! Smash white supremacy! Occupy the schools!

With a similarly provocative spirit, we might consider even more cosmic questions:

* What does it mean to be human right now, today?

* How can we act ethically in our hurried, off-balance, and bewildering world?
* How did we get here, and where do we want to go?
* What is our map of the known world, and how might it look if we rethought it from top to bottom and redrew all the lines?
* What is our responsibility as world citizens to one another and to future generations?
* What kind of society do we want to inhabit?
* What is the relationship of democracy to economics?
* Who do we want to be as people? What can we become?
* What gives meaning to our lives?

"All's well," says the town crier making rounds through the village and lighting lamps for the night. Perhaps it's simply a reassuring thought for the townspeople, or perhaps there's a more malevolent message, the toxic propaganda that the status quo is inevitable and that there is no alternative to the way things are. The dissident, the artist, the agitator, the dreamer, and the activist respond, "No, all is not well." The current moment is neither immutable nor inescapable, and its imperfections are cause for general alarm—for the exploited and the oppressed the status quo is itself an ongoing act of violence.

Activists announce through their lives and their work that a new world is in the making. We can create a community of agitators and transform this corner of the world into a place that we *want* to inhabit. We can identify ourselves as citizens of a country that does not yet exist and has no map, and become that new nation's pioneers and cartographers—and through our common actions bring a more assertive and vibrant public into being.

Each of us is immersed in what is, the world as such. In order to link arms and rise up we need a combination of somethings: seeds, surely; desire, perhaps; a vision of community and possibility; necessity and even, at times, desperation; willful enthusiasm and an acceptance that there are no guarantees whatsoever.

Imagination is indispensable in these efforts and pursuits because it "ignites the slow fuse of possibility," as Emily Dickinson wrote. More process than product, more stance than conclusion, engaging the imagination involves the dynamic work of igniting that fuse, mapping the world as it really is, and then purposely stepping outside and leaning toward a possible world.

We may accept our lot in life as inevitable for decades, generations, even centuries, but when fresh and startling winds begin to blow and revolution is in the air, when a lovelier life comes into view for masses of people and a possible world becomes vaguely and then acutely visible—glimpses of which fill the pages that follow—at that moment, the status quo becomes suddenly, shockingly unendurable. This is the moment when we reject the fixed and the stable and begin to reach for alternatives. The imagination erupts. And nourishing our radical imaginations means traveling to the root of things, seeking causes and connections, while simultaneously struggling in the here and now for relatively more peace and equality, comparatively more joy and justice, an expanded field of hope.

Hope and fierce collective determination are choices; confidence is a politics. We don't want to minimize the horror, but neither do we want to be sucked into its thrall. Hope is an antidote to cynicism and despair; it's the capacity to notice or invent alternatives; it's nourishing the precious sense that standing directly against the world *as such* is a world that *could* be, or *should* be. Whatever *is* the case stands side by side with what *could* be or *should* be the case. Without that vital sense of possibility, doors close, curtains drop, and we become stuck: we cannot adequately oppose injustice; we cannot act freely; we cannot inhabit the most vigorous moral spaces. We are never freer, all of us and each of us, than when we refuse the situations before us as settled and certain and determined—the absolute end of the matter—and break the chains that entangle us, launching ourselves toward the imaginable.

We need to make a distinction between personal virtues— be honest, do your work, and show up on time—and social or community ethics. Personal virtue is surely good, but we would be hard pressed to say that a slave owner who paid the bills on time and was loyal or kind to the children was an ethical person—the blithe indifference to the larger social context allows the rotten system itself to thrive. We need to think about how we act customarily and collectively, how our society functions, how the contexts of politics and culture and economics, for example, interact with what we hold to be good, and how an ethical society allows more of us more of the time to act ethically. Most of us, after all, mostly follow the prevailing conventions of our time and place—most Spartans acted like Spartans; most Athenians, like Athenians; and most North Americans, even those in quite different economic and social circumstances, and for better and for worse, act most often like North Americans. To be an ethical actor and a person of moral character in an unjust social order requires something more: to work in common to change that society, to rewrite its rules and its narrative, to come together with others in order to rise up and resist. It requires activists and agitators and artists and dissidents willing to take risks on behalf of something better. It's obvious now (even if it was obscure to many people then) that the good people and the moral actors in the days of American slavery were the runaways who exercised their agency in courageous and surprising acts of self-liberation and the abolitionists who joined the cause. When the system of slavery was legally abolished, a new moral norm was established, and everyone, acting normally, was freed to discover the better angels of themselves.

What if we took another leap forward, and agreed that predation and exploitation were unacceptable? What if the vast majority of people mobilized to abolish the system of private profit and wage slavery altogether? What if the horizon of our moral universe stretched that far? What could we imagine then, and what might we build together?

Human beings are driven by a long and continuous "I don't know, and I'd like to find out." It's not the known that propels us out of bed and out the door, it's not the status quo that prods us up the next hill or onto the next challenge, nor is it "received wisdom" that pushes and pulls us along. Rather, the deep motivation at the core of our humanity, the powerful force pushing toward enlightenment and liberation, is the hope that we will once again create and invent, plant and build, challenge and overcome.

This is a call to resist the insistent pull of tradition or dogma, the easy acquiescence to the orthodox opinion of the moment. It's an argument against the cynical shrug that says, "That's just the way things are," and the world-weary sigh that implies that nothing can be done. This is a manifesto against passivity and defeat, and in favor of action as an antidote to despair. This is an invitation to gather together in an expanding public square, hand in hand, shoulder to shoulder, in order to fight for something radically different and dramatically better.

History has surprised us before, and history can surely surprise us again.

What if?

One

Military-Industrial Complex Index

Year the United States established what
would become a standing army: 1940

Rank of United States in military spending worldwide: 1

Percent of world's total military budget: 34

Percent increase in US military spending between
1998 and 2011 (in constant 2011 dollars): 88

Total US military spending annually
(in 2014): $609,914,000,000

Minimum number of US military
bases in foreign countries: 587

Number of foreign military installations
based on US territory: 0

Amount of money to private defense corporations
in FY 2015: $272,790,578,374

Percent to top five contractors in 2015: 27

Rank of United States as a global arms dealer (2015): 1

A pervasive and frantically promoted proposition that runs loose in the land is that being a military powerhouse makes the United States (and people everywhere) safe, protects freedoms, and is a force for peace and democracy in a threatening, dangerous, and hostile world. It's not true—not even close—but it has a huge and sticky hold on our imaginations.

When a random US politician tells antiwar protesters picketing a town hall meeting, "It's because of the sacrifices our troops are making in [fill in the blank: Iraq, Afghanistan, Syria, Yemen, Libya, the "Middle East," Korea, Panama, or wherever turns out to be next] that you have the freedom to stand here and speak out," s/he is tapping into that stuttering cliché. When a retired general speaks confidently at a televised congressional hearing, explaining to the credulous audience that the "enemy can be defeated" if only the Pentagon would be granted more funds to purchase more weapons, and then given greater leeway in their deployment and use, he's issuing the same unexamined and banal truism. When a talking head tells us it's unfortunate that US economic strength rides on oil, a resource that "happens to come from a nasty neighborhood," but it's "a blessing" we have the power to police that part of the world, s/he's doing the same thing. And when folks across the political spectrum express public gratitude and support for "our fighting men and women overseas," while refusing to send their own children into those same wars or harboring serious private doubts about the wisdom, purpose, and execution of whatever US adventure is currently in play, they too are situated in that wide open field of received wisdom and diminishing options.

What if we challenged these instances of hypocrisy and defensive dogma, and insisted that there are more honest and straightforward ways to support US military men and women? What if we demanded their immediate decommission and return home, and insisted that they be provided excellent medical and psychological care, good jobs, affordable housing, and the best available educational opportunities—the things every human being deserves? What if we spoke up in the face of that woolly politician and asked him to draw a straight line between free speech and the specific invasion he's now supporting and explicitly (or at least implicitly) defending? What if we locked arms as we built a growing wave of peace advocates, anticipating and opposing the next aggression, and the next?

Dramatically rethinking the manufactured rationale for war, reframing it, and turning it upside-down brings us closer to the truth: The massive US military-industrial powerhouse and increasingly privatized war machine makes North Americans (and everyone else) unsafe in the world, undermines human security and hard-won rights and freedoms, and is the greatest purveyor of violence on Earth.

The history of US military actions is a history of conquest and genocide from the start and chaos and catastrophe ever since: invading and occupying Vietnam and then intentionally expanding that war into neighboring Laos and Cambodia as retribution for the US defeat, a disaster that cost the lives of six thousand people every week for ten years; unleashing a massive shock-and-awe attack on Iraq in 2003 that led to the breakup of that nation and the rise of several reactionary fundamentalist and terrorist formations including ISIS; orchestrating a fifty-year campaign to destabilize and topple the Cuban government; propping up nasty regimes from medieval Saudi Arabia to apartheid South Africa; overthrowing elected presidents in Iran in 1953, Guatemala in 1954, and Chile in 1973; instigating constant civil unrest in Venezuela, for fourteen years including a successful if short-lived coup in 2002; supporting the communist purge and the genocide that followed in Indonesia in the mid-1960s; participating in the murders of the African freedom fighter Patrice Lumumba in Congo in 1961, the Moroccan anti-imperialist Mehdi Ben Barka in Paris in 1965, the internationalist Che Guevara in Bolivia in 1967, and the anticolonial leader Amílcar Cabral in Guinea-Bissau in 1973; exporting billions of dollars in arms to Israel, Turkey, and Saudi Arabia, and reactionary regimes and right-wing subversives the world around. As busy and ambitious as this looks, it's only the tip of a menacing mega-iceberg, an emblematic list as opposed to an exhaustive survey.

My list so far doesn't include the "war on terror" launched in 2001, the subsequent invasions of Afghanistan and Iraq, the bombing campaigns that followed in Yemen, Syria, Pakistan, Afghanistan, and Libya, the creation of robot warriors and a unique modern evil called drone warfare as a preferred tactic for delivering massive violence abroad while muting objections at home, the steady spread of offensive US military power in all directions—this never-ending turmoil raises troubling questions: Are the architects of this madness crazy or are they stupid? Are they banal or evil? Is the real goal, in spite of whatever lofty rhetoric about democracy and freedom is on offer, to break things up and smash cities and states to smithereens intentionally? Maybe pandemonium and extensive wreckage are not unintended consequences but represent, instead, "mission accomplished." Maybe the masters of war expect that at the end of the day there will be no opposing organized armed forces left, lots of rebuilding contracts to give away to their billionaire pals, and plentiful oil or other resources there for the taking.

In any case, the swirling vortex of ruin obscures for many North Americans a central source and seed of this overwhelming maelstrom of hostility and bloodshed: the indefensible relationship between the United States and its chief client, Israel. Israel, as everyone knows, was established in 1948 by a people who had experienced the lash of anti-Semitism for centuries and the immediate colossal horrors of the Holocaust in Europe. What's often conveniently understated or downplayed in the United States, however, is that while understandably wanting to create a refuge for themselves, the founders of the state of Israel dislodged the indigenous inhabitants and destroyed their society, forcing them to become displaced persons and refugees or second-class citizens in their own land ever since.

With generous and unwavering support from the United States, its protector, enabler, and big brother, Israel has flouted UN resolutions and international law—including nuclear agreements, the Geneva conventions, and the "laws of war"—seized Palestinian land and zealously supported the settler movement in the occupied territories with infrastructure and violent force. Israel would stand completely alone in the world if not for the dysfunctional relationship it clings to with the United States—from which it gains billions of dollars in military aid alone.

The Palestinians have the ongoing misfortune of being the victims of the twentieth century's most notable victims—whose exceptional suffering at the hands of the Nazis is consistently trotted out to justify Israel's own crimes against humanity. Reactionaries who dream of a Greater Israel, a Promised Land stretching from the Nile to the Euphrates, plot and organize the elimination of all Palestinians one way or another. Under the banner of agony and pain, Israel unleashes murderous military attacks and conducts massive ethnic cleansing campaigns. And yet the reality on the ground is that the Palestinians and the Israeli Jews are so intertwined that there is no separation between them except for the separation of apartheid—two populations living in one land, unequal today, but not necessarily forever.

The appalling codependency between the United States and Israel is one root cause of the world's suffering, and another is the deployment of its "global basing strategy" in which the United States maintains nuclear warheads in the air at all times, hides CIA agents in every embassy and behind every tree, spies on everyone everywhere all the time, and sends hundreds of thousands of "fighting men and women overseas" as today's Spartans. That strategy leads to no lasting solutions. On the contrary, the rise of this domineering nexus creates a culture of fear and social paranoia, encourages deception, dishonesty, and militarism, places the economy in the precarious position of adjunct and subsidiary to the Pentagon, undermines the moral landscape, and enriches a few as it devastates the lives of millions.

What if seeing this deadly display allows us to discuss war and military might on an entirely different terrain? Could we then come closer to matching our reality with our predicament? What if we echoed Iraq Veterans Against the War: not another drop of blood or another wasted dollar on the "war on terror" or the imperial dreams of the 1 percent? Endless war only deepens the catastrophe and suspends or destroys the possibility of reimagining and rebuilding the United States as a more peaceful, joyous, just, participatory, and cooperative place.

This reimagining taps into plain sense: we want to be good and peaceful people, to be kind and generous and neighborly, to do unto others as we would have them do unto us. The Warrior is not the only American archetype; there is also the Hard Worker, the Good Farmer, the Peace Lover, and the Free Thinker. Two histories, two aspects of the American experience, two spirits in our collective psyche: fighter/peacemaker, trooper/bridge-builder, soldier-at-arms/pacifist. When we reframe the discussion this way, we can dive headfirst into the contradictions, fully engaging that deeply contested space.

Veterans for Peace has thousands of members in chapters from coast to coast and around the globe who call in one unified and rising voice for an end to war: "We, having dutifully served our nation, do hereby affirm our greater responsibility to serve the cause of world peace."

Their message is spare and unadorned: abolish war as an instrument of international policy; end the arms race and eliminate nuclear weapons; restrain the government from intervening in the affairs of other nations; support universal principles of nonintervention and self-determination; work for human security not national security; increase public awareness of the various and sundry costs of war. In other words, abrogate the military contract in favor of a moral social contract.

Antiwar vets bring a laser-like clarity to war's perverse and seductive qualities, its myths versus its monstrous reality, and to the ambivalence and conflicted responses returning vets face at home. Like Odysseus, literature's most famous returning veteran, both war and the journey home are marked by obstacles and challenges, and most often characterized by brutal remembrances of things lost. Lost comrades, lost time, and lost childhoods; loss of a family one once knew; loss of a sturdy sense of well-being; loss of the sweet dreams of youth when everything seemed possible. Veterans can easily feel like dislocated strangers in their own lands: no one and nothing remains quite the same. And like every generation of fighters since Odysseus 2,800 years ago they know too well the emotional trauma and mental shards that travel home with them. Suffering with what was once called "shell shock" or "battle fatigue" (or less generously "irritable heart" and "malingering"), today's veterans have experienced up close that universal creature whose name has morphed into a sanitized, technologically appointed, and contemporary medical condition, irritable heart with a scientific shine: post-traumatic stress syndrome.

In 2004 a group of young people founded Iraq Veterans Against the War (IVAW), and a month later mustered a small but spirited contingent to march in New York City at the Republican National Convention. Their name emblazoned on a banner brought wild applause and cheering wherever they went in those few days. By the end of the summer their membership had swelled to fifty.

Its numbers have exploded since then. Search for a chapter in your neighborhood; seek out a member. You will likely find— as I have again and again—a person whose rhetoric is strictly no-bullshit and whose message is punctuated with passion and urgency. These are multiracial, multi-ethnic women and men of every creed and every age and background whose stance echoes perhaps the best line from the film *Avatar*: "I didn't sign up for this shit." Each wants to share with the rest of us the difficult and necessary lessons they've learned—there's no time to waste with frothy rhetoric. They intend, as well, to shoulder what they take to be a sacred duty: representing their fallen comrades who believed—incorrectly it turns out—that their sacrifices would advance toward peace. Their zeal is forged in the furnaces of war; their fire is tempered with experiences of pain and loss, self-sacrifice and loyalty, endurance and courage. They demand to be heard.

The members of Vietnam Veterans Against the War (VVAW) were brave and lucid in their quest for peace in the 1970s. They told the truth about the reality of invasion and occupation, about war crimes committed daily by US air strikes and bombardments and ground troops, about the big lies that led to and then perpetuated the war. They also recognized immediately that the US defeat in Vietnam was not all bad—which is worse for the world, after all, an aggressive, imperial army triumphant or an invading army defeated? The defeat was humbling but at the same time humanizing for the troops and for society as a whole at a certain moment—it provided a space of clarity and grace.

Imagine the force that we would unleash if hundreds of thousands of young people gave up their weapons of war and redeployed their intelligence and their energy to build bridges, repair roads, improve the housing stock across the country; to work with youth in athletic and arts programs; to care for the elderly and the very young; to staff emergency rooms; to create urban farms and rural performance spaces. Imagine who we could become if the Warrior transformed into the Teacher and the Caregiver and the Farmer.

The masters of the Pentagon, insisting that the United States didn't "lose Vietnam," but rather chickened out, learned a different set of lessons, of course, and came to a different set of conclusions: First, a citizen army is not feasible for a country bent on permanent war because citizens have the irritating habit of occasionally thinking for themselves, saying or doing the most outrageous things like collectively resisting illegal and immoral actions. Second, a free press—which may act as a public relations arm of nationalistic war-mongering much of the time, but in an era of defeat may ask inconvenient questions and uncover damning truths—must never be allowed unfettered access to a US battlefield. Lo and behold: A citizen army becomes a relic of the past, replaced by a professional (with many features of a mercenary) army; the old selective service system is replaced with an "economic draft"; and since 1975 no establishment, for-profit media conglomerate has sent reporters to a US war zone without a military minder.

I remember a young, war-weary John Kerry testifying in front of the Senate upon his return from war saying that the US military committed war crimes in Vietnam every day, not as a matter of choice but as a matter of policy. An older John Kerry, secretary of state in the second term of a war-hungry administration, denounced Russia's intervention in Crimea, saying in effect that it's inappropriate to invade another country in order to force your will on people at the end of a barrel of a gun. Though the mainstream media failed to point out the breathtaking hypocrisy of this scolding from a high US official, Stephen Colbert gave Secretary Kerry a congratulatory "tip of the hat" when he played the full clip, gestured sternly, and said, "Starting now!"

In the empire of lies, every truth-teller is a traitor; in the United States of Amnesia, memory is the first casualty.

Justice and democracy do not belong to war; on the contrary, each is easily injured and quickly exterminated in its furnaces. John Dewey observed that "All nations, even those professedly the most democratic," are compelled in war "to turn authoritarian and totalitarian."[1] We can see the wreckage all around us: omnivorous national security and surveillance; the abrogation of privacy and civil liberties; the wide use of mass incarceration; the banality of torture, domestically and internationally; and the undermining of tolerance everywhere. Historically, law and rights yield in the face of war: Abraham Lincoln's famous suspension of habeas corpus during the Civil War; the Palmer Raids following World War I; the mass arrests and incarceration of Japanese Americans during World War II; illegal imprisonment as policy today. These moves are all defended by the war-makers as necessary during wartime.

Since 9/11 the United States has entered new territory, for we are in our fifteenth year of a government-proclaimed state of *permanent* war, an absolute war against "terrorism" or "evil." While there are indeed dreadful and desperate tactics being deployed everywhere—suicide bombings, hijackings, beheadings, random killings—the enemy remains vague and the target elusive: terrorists and "evildoers," insurgents and radicals, the "worst of the worst" or the "bad actors." Practically every politician in Washington notes casually that we are *at war*; it's completely normalized. George W. Bush proudly called himself a "war president"; Barack Obama too chose to claim the mantle of the warrior. Whoever sits on the throne of American Empire wears the garments of the warmonger— unless and until we bring the power of a popular movement to bear down and end imperialism altogether.

Imagine if every "known terrorist" were dead or in prison. Now try to imagine the state announcing an end to airport searches and phone taps. It's inconceivable.

Ask one of our careless politicians how we will know if any given war is won, or what the benchmarks of success or failure might be, and they become speechless. For these are perpetual wars, wars without borders, without obvious or easily defined enemies, and without concrete objectives; we can only know they are over when our Dear Leaders tell us they're over. Until then—and don't hold your breath—your rights to free speech and association are suspended because the rulers want to keep you safe, and these measures, they assure us, are an unfortunate necessity of war.

* * *

Private Chelsea Manning (formerly Bradley Manning) is a US soldier who was isolated in a military dungeon at Marine Corps Base Quantico in Virginia for the crime of truth-telling. She was denied exercise, given no pillow or sheets for the bed, and, while on "suicide watch," fed antidepressants by military doctors as government agents tried to erase her mind, destroy her spirit, and obliterate any sense of agency. It's reminiscent of the heartless torturer in *1984* who explains to Winston what will happen to him: "Never again will you be capable of ordinary human feeling. Everything will be dead inside you. Never again will you be capable of love, or friendship, or joy of living, or laughter, or curiosity, or courage, or integrity. You will be hollow. We shall squeeze you empty and then we shall fill you with ourselves."

The US government fell over itself to demonize and misdirect, portraying Private Manning as a nut and a repressed homosexual. It labeled Julian Assange, WikiLeaks founder and public face, a terrorist, enemy combatant, and irresponsible saboteur, and threatened everything from assassination to charges of espionage and high treason. When anyone is in the crosshairs of the most powerful empire on Earth, everything said about them should be taken with a truckload of salt.

The United States never answers the question of why, in a putative democracy, all the WikiLeaks material was classified to begin with. Nor does it address the content of the documents, the dark and dirty secrets of the war-makers, the cozy "don't ask, don't tell" relationships with the nastiest dictators on Earth, the stunning violence and the cold rationalizations, or the murderousness followed by lies, deception, and cover-ups. The US government never faces the most obvious and damning truth of the whole affair: we live in a barricaded, secret society, a garrison state that supports and is supported by a powerfully developed culture of war.

Umberto Eco who, after noting that the Orwellian prophecy is realized once power can monitor with a watchful eye the total movement of every citizen, raised a cheer for the secrecy pirates and the hackers of WikiLeaks because "the surveillance ceases to work only one way" and "the citizens' self-appointed avenger" can open the crypts of state secrets.[2]

When in 2014 a federal judge sentenced Jeremy Hammond to ten years in prison for his work with the hacking network Anonymous, she referenced the Vietnam-era Pentagon Papers whistleblower Daniel Ellsberg (a Jeremy supporter who exposed the lies that were used to prop up support for the war in Vietnam in the 1960s) as she scolded from the bench. "You're no Daniel Ellsberg," she intoned, forgetting that Daniel Ellsberg was no "Daniel Ellsberg" when he was in fact Daniel Ellsberg; back then he was demonized, systematically harassed, threatened, arrested, charged under the Espionage Act, and put on trial, facing 115 years in prison.

Edward Snowden, the latest avenger of the people, offered secret classified documents taken from the National Security Agency to journalists working at mainstream news organizations; several, including the *New York Times*, the *Guardian*, and *Der Speigel*, chose to publish parts of those documents over several months. Snowden fled the country to Hong Kong, and later Moscow, as he was denounced in Congress from all sides, put on trial by the corporate media, and called a traitor, a spy, a lowlife. Perhaps he was no Daniel Ellsberg either, but his courageous actions put him well on his way to becoming as iconic and important now as Ellsberg was then.

As a little blue-sky exercise, imagine any bit of the war culture transformed into a peace-and-love culture: the Super Bowl opening with thousands of local school kids rushing through the stands distributing their poetry, and then everyone singing "This Land Is Your Land" or "Give Peace a Chance," or "We Shall Overcome"; an airlines or bus terminal clerk saying, "We want to invite any teachers or nurses in the gate area to board first, and we thank you for your service"; urban high schools eliminating ROTC and banning military recruiters in favor of school-wide assemblies for peace recruiters featuring Code Pink, and after-school programs led by Black Youth Project 100 and the American Friends Service Committee.

Like every culture or subculture, the war culture hangs together with a complex set of shared meanings, webs of significance and common assumptions woven in such a way that members of the culture can communicate with and recognize one another. The war culture promotes a pervasive and growing common sense of American violence unleashed.

The United States spends more than a trillion dollars a year on war and preparation for war, more than the rest of the world combined. The war culture accepts that as a desire for peace. The United States has military bases stretching across the globe, including a base in the Italian Alps, and yet there are no Italian air bases in the Catskills, for example. The war culture sees that as sensible and necessary. The war culture is everywhere, simply taken for granted, always lurking in the shadows and occasionally bursting forth and on full display.

I remember a trailer for a film I saw in a theater several years ago—it looked dreadful, so I never saw the film, but it could well have been *Mars Attacks* or *The Day the Earth Stood Still*—in which the repeating trope was an alien confronting a group of startled Earthlings, saying in an eerily mechanical voice, "We come in peace"—just before blasting them into small pieces. It takes a minute for reality to catch up to these hapless Earthlings, but eventually they get it. Like the challenge of the wandering spouse caught in the arms of a lover, the aliens hold to the classic defense, "Who are you going to believe, me or your own lying eyes?"

This is precisely the situation the United States finds itself in all over the world: We come in peace. We *always* come in peace. But let us ask the youth in the streets of Cairo or Tunis facing US arms in the hands of American-financed dictators, or the women servicing the US military bases stretching across their landscapes, or the farmers and workers all over Latin America, Africa, and Asia whose repressive police forces and militias are trained and supplied by US aid, or any people anywhere who find themselves in the sights of an

American-made rocket or a US drone: What are you going to believe? Your own lying eyes?

In our stuttering mechanical message we announce to ourselves and to everyone else that we are a peaceful people, our intentions always righteous and just. It's comforting, and it's a deeply held self-description, so compelling that it rises quickly to the status of common sense, requiring no investigation, no fact-checking, no external validation whatsoever. All right-thinking people believe it; everyone simply *knows* that it's true.

On any given week you can read or hear the words of a surprised soldier in a US-occupied land saying, "We came to help, but a lot of people don't seem to like us," or, "The hardest thing is figuring out who our friends are and who the enemy is among the locals—they smile at you one minute, and toss a bomb the next." There's a kind of willful innocence and self-inflicted or forced blindness at work here, for these are the exact words of the British colonial militiaman in India or the French soldier in occupied Algeria or Indochina, the theme song of the troops in every conquering army since time began. See the pictures of US troops searching a home looking for "bad guys" or "insurgents" or "terrorists" in any recent theater of war; take the perspective for a moment of the women watching from the corner, huddled with their terrorized children.

"We come in peace," but wherever the United States puts down the boot, it brings more war, wider war, and a deeper commitment to war as the way. Marine Corps major general Smedley Butler, two-time winner of the Congressional Medal of Honor, said in 1935 that "War is a racket." That was the title of a popular pamphlet he wrote, and a theme he elaborated in speeches throughout the country over many years: "It always has been. It is possibly the oldest, easily the most profitable, surely the most vicious. . . . It is the only one in which the profits are reckoned in dollars and the losses in lives."[3] Butler consistently urged citizens to demand the impossible and support three radical proposals: strictly limit all military forces to a defensive posture; hold a referendum of those who would be on the front lines before any military action is undertaken; and take the profit out of war by, among other measures, conscripting the captains of industry and finance as the foot soldiers in any impending fight.

Years later, in his farewell address to the nation, President Dwight D. Eisenhower, a career soldier and supreme Allied commander during World War II, warned of the "unwarranted influence, whether sought or unsought," of a voracious and dangerous "military-industrial complex," and "a permanent armaments industry of vast proportions" capable of undermining the institutions and culture of democracy. The "conjunction of an immense military establishment and a large arms industry is new in the American experience," he said, and its "total influence—economic, political, even spiritual—is felt in every city, every State house, every office of the Federal government." He predicted "the disastrous rise of misplaced power" unless Americans refused and resisted it, and committed themselves instead to working "in the interests of world peace and human betterment."[4]

Fifty years after this most-famous cautionary message the permanent war economy is well established and interwoven with all other aspects of our lives. Eisenhower's speculation concerning a shadowy agenda promoted by an all-powerful, corporatized military has been realized: torture at Abu Ghraib and Guantánamo; "black sites" for CIA special rendition cases; warrantless wiretaps; multiyear military detentions without due process; surveillance cameras everywhere; and growing banks of fingerprints, eye scans, and DNA samples. This is a description of what is. This is here; it is us.

To hope for a world at peace and in balance, powered by love, joy, and justice, to insist that the citizens and residents of the United States become a people among people (not a superior or a chosen people) and that the country becomes a nation among nations (not some kind of crypto-fascist *übernation*) is to resist the logic and the reality of war, and to see, as well, the war culture itself as a site of resistance and transformation. It's to break with the frame that acts as if war is natural and inevitable. It's to do the hard work of making a vibrant and robust peace movement—connecting with the environmental activists, the immigrant rights forces, the Black Lives Matter upsurge, feminists, and the queer movement—organizing to close all US military bases abroad and to bring all troops home now, leaving no US military or paid mercenaries behind; compelling our government to sign all pending international treaties on nuclear disarmament; mobilizing to cut military spending by 10 percent a year for the next ten years, dedicating the savings to education and health; rallying to suspend and then abrogate all contracts between the US government and Halliburton, Lockheed Martin, and Northrop Grumman.

We come together, then, to unleash our wild and free imaginations—our art and humor and creative energies—to defeat the plodding, murderous, and instrumentalist logic of war. Theirs is a calculus of conquest and pain. Ours offers a measure of healing and possibility.

Two

Prison Complex Index

Change in the rate of incarceration in the
past forty years (1972–2012): + 439%

Rank of a metaphorical "Correctional Supervision
City" by population for all US cities (2014): 2

Rank of the US incarcerated population in the
world (most recent figures for all countries): 1

Percent of all of the world's prisoners in US prisons
(most recent figures for all countries): 21

Percent of Americans engaged in "guard labor"—
defending property, supervising work, or otherwise
keeping their fellow Americans in line (2002): 26.1

Rate of juveniles detained in the United States to all
comparison nations combined (US figures from 2006): 5.5:1

Average annual cost to keep a juvenile in detention
in the United States in 2011: $148,767

Average annual cost per child to fund
US schools, 2010–2011: $12,926

Year that the US Supreme Court ruled that solitary
confinement caused prisoners to fall into "a semi-fatuous
condition, from which it was next to impossible to arouse
them, and others became violently insane": 1890

Estimated number of inmates in solitary confinement
in "supermax" prisons (2005): 25,000

Neither slavery nor involuntary servitude, except as a punishment for crime whereof the party shall have been duly convicted, shall exist within the United States, or any place subject to their jurisdiction.

—Thirteenth Amendment to the US
Constitution (1865), Section 1

Say what? Slavery and involuntary servitude were abolished in 1865 "except as a punishment for crime?" So if a person has been legally convicted of crime, he or she could again be enslaved or forced into involuntary servitude, according to the US Constitution. That helps explain the creepy feeling I've always had whenever I'm in or even near a prison: the stench of the slave market in the air, and the specter of the plantation hovering everywhere. In many places the prison/ plantations didn't even bother changing their names: Angola Plantation in Louisiana became Angola Prison, Parchman Farm is still Parchman Farm. The language remained intact, and so did the deeper political structure.

While the Emancipation Proclamation of 1863 freed the enslaved workers of the Confederacy, and then when slavery was formally finished in the United States in 1865, life remained treacherous and unstable for the formerly enslaved people for many reasons, not least that crafty loophole: *except as a punishment for crime.* With the withdrawal of federal troops and the defeat of Black Reconstruction the former slave-holding states quickly passed laws—the infamous Black Codes that existed for over a century—designed to criminalize Black life and give the white establishment an easy pass to continued supremacy, domination, indentured servitude, and exploitation. These laws then combined with hastily instituted Jim Crow practices—racial segregation, the mass campaign of terror, the regime of lynching, disenfranchisement, and a system of peonage that entrapped workers in debt and forced them to labor indefinitely as peasants or serfs within a system of bondage—officially conformed to the new order of life-without-slavery, while undermining it in every detail and reasserting white supremacy and state control of Black bodies with a vengeance.

In Mississippi, for example, formerly enslaved people could be sentenced to forced labor for crimes including petty theft, using obscene language, or selling cotton after sunset. It's an old tradition, tried and true: The law, in all its majesty and even-handed equanimity, censures rich and poor alike if they're found begging on the public streets or stealing bread or sleeping under the highway bridges. An 1865 law titled "An Act to Confer Civil Rights on Freedmen" required Black workers to contract with white farmers by January 1 of each year or face punishment for vagrancy. Chain gangs and work camps sprang up everywhere as the labor of these "duly convicted" former chattels was sold to farms, factories, quarries, and mines. The workers on the chain gangs were no longer a part of the slave system, but of an easily recognizable twin: involuntary servitude as a result of being duly convicted of crime. Same work, same workers, new label.

We begin to see clearly the tough bond of white supremacy over changing times and reorganized systems, the thick white glob of glue binding slavery to Jim Crow and then to prisons, bondage, and mass incarceration. The slave system and the mass incarceration system each violently subordinate subjugated persons to the will of their masters; each insists that subjects follow strict routines dictated by the rulers; each reduces subjects to dependency for everything including food and shelter; each isolates its subjects from normal human contact or intercourse; and each forces subjects to work for minimal compensation.

Both systems comprehensively create an identifiable lower caste. Today that caste is racially coded but not explicitly race identified, which means that folks can be victimized and legally discriminated against in a wide range of ways: the criminal caste often cannot vote or serve on a jury, live in specific places, access student and other forms of loans, or hold a wide range of jobs. In 2004 more Black people were disenfranchised than in 1870, and 5.3 million citizens suffer this specific civic death penalty now.

✳ ✳ ✳

For the oppressors and the exploiting class, there's a ready rationale in every age: from the start white supremacy was promoted to justify aggression, theft, occupation, kidnapping, and murder—it was never based on inferiority, real or imagined. Racism has been aggressively employed in the service of cheap labor and in the suppression of wages and the precariousness of workers' status, and racism justified colonial plunder from the start. As the US Empire began its long and dangerous decline and the industrial heartland collapsed in the middle of the twentieth century, creating excess labor became a fearsome predicament for the rulers. The Black freedom movement pushed forward at the same time, demanding access, recognition, and equality. But the counterrevolution pushed back—the gains of African Americans were nominally accepted as an accomplished fact, but in reality they were challenged, halted, and reversed wherever possible. When overt bigotry became socially unacceptable to many, coded markers—crime, drugs, violence—took its place. With African Americans on the march and revolution in the air, with unemployment soaring and jobs disappearing, prison became a central strategy to address multiple crises.

Like the Black Codes decades ago, a wide range of laws, practices, and traditions from mandatory minimum sentences to cash bail feed the prison and criminal caste systems. Stop-and-frisk policies in New York City for years led to young Black men having contact with the police in wildly disproportionate numbers; young African American men in

Chicago are three times more likely to be taken to a police station for a curfew violation than their white counterparts; Black boys are twice as likely as white boys to be suspended or expelled from high school; disparate sentencing practices for the same or similar drug possessions result in African Americans being twice as likely as others to do time; in Ferguson the practice of imposing fines on Black residents to fill the city's coffers has been widely scrutinized; in Chicago where police have discretion to ticket or arrest someone in possession of marijuana, Black people have accounted for 95 percent of those particular arrests over the past four years.

All of this is racism in operation, and it's worth noting here that the word "racism" has multiple meanings. In popular usage it means bigotry, often manifest in ignorant comments, stereotyped views, and backward language. For example, Cliven Bundy, the cattle rancher from Nevada, is a racist—just listen to him and you know he's an offensive bigot. And since you and I aren't bigots, we can glibly claim the high moral ground. But there's a problem: "racism" is also the structures of white supremacy and the institutional practices of oppression based on race. The examples above are instances of the execution of institutional racism. And so the question for antiracists isn't, "Are you a bigot?" but "What are you doing to attack the institutional expressions of white supremacy?" The mayor of Chicago shuttered more than fifty public schools in predominantly Black communities and never used the N-word; a slick, sophisticated, and charming president pushed harsh legislation that resulted in mass incarceration and the overrepresentation of Black people in prisons. This is white supremacy, and racist practice on the ground and in the world. Call its name.

I've been to jail myself—arrested for sit-ins, blockades around buildings, and other acts of civil disobedience as well as "disorderly conduct" and "mob action" and "disturbing the peace"—and I'm not done yet. Of course my (mostly voluntary) encounters with the criminal justice system are vastly different from the encounters of a young, impoverished Black man—I encounter the system from a position of relative power, and I make no comparisons between myself and most of those caught up in the system. I navigate the cruel intricacies of the system from a place of privilege. Still as Thoreau so perfectly pointed out, in a war-making slave state (in his day) or a racist, war-making punishing state (in our own), an appropriate place for a free and honest person is in jail.

I've never lived in a prison, however, only visited, and always under heartbreaking circumstances: my partner, Bernardine Dohrn, held in federal lockup for months for refusing to participate in a star-chamber grand jury; David Gilbert, the other father of our adopted son Chesa, is in his thirty-fifth year in the New York State prison system doing a seventy-five-years-to-life bid; and Kathy Boudin, David's partner and Chesa's other mother, did twenty-two years in prison of a twenty-years-to-life sentence. Kathy was supremely fortunate to have gotten out at all, and since her release she's been a marvel of good work—an extension, really, of the dazzling organizing she did while inside for family rights, decent health care, and access to education. We've spent hours, days, and weekends with them sharing space and time and life in whatever nasty medieval dungeon they were caged in at the time, and we've lived the prison experience vicariously—as millions of other family members have—for decades.

Visiting David recently, I walked into the visitor's entrance, the guards checked my ID and asked me to sign in, first in the log book, then again at the main prison building, and finally at the check-in desk in the visiting room itself. I walked through a metal detector and had my hand stamped with ultraviolet ink, which was then scanned as I passed through a series of gates that were opened sequentially by someone in an unseen command center on my way to the visiting room. I finally sat at a small round table under the eyes of two guards on a raised platform and, I thought, several cameras installed in the ceiling. This is all standard procedure for entering a maximum-security prison—no surprises—and also a vivid reminder that to be ruled is to be regulated and checked off, ordered about and counted, noted and routinely observed. We were on the far end away from freedom, to be sure.

David is always remarkably calm and thoughtful and centered when we visit, always a reminder that every human being, no matter the circumstances, has some agency to call upon and exercise. I often wonder if I could achieve anything approaching his productivity and his Yoda-like attitude and focus while in the midst of the bedlam swirling around us—the raw reunions, the broken parents and sobbing family members, the wriggling, sometimes stressed-out kids, the high drama of these few moments of face-to-face relations followed by seemingly endless stretches of separation, the palpable tension of connecting under the watchful eyes of the keepers. The constant noise, the stale air and unnatural light, the vending machines offering a steady fare of grease and sugar, the tough feel of concrete and metal—it all conspires to diminish and erase the competing energy: humanity itself, trembling and real.

The experience of prison is one of powerlessness and confrontation, petty humiliation and shaming, isolation and individualization. The authorities have no tolerance for collective voices or community action—you must be all alone all the time—and so the escalation of noise, distraction, confrontation, and violence is built into the structure and the environment itself.

I often tried to provoke my students at the University of Illinois at Chicago by saying, "Do you know that one mile from our campus there are 15,000 Irishmen [or Jewish women, or Greeks] living in cages?" "Come on! No way!" There was always a general sense of disbelief, and a notion that maybe I was joking. "You're kidding, right?"

Well, yes and no: I wasn't being fully honest, so let me change it a bit—"Do you know that one mile from our campus there are 15,000 young Black and Latino men living in cages?" "No, I didn't know that, but I'm not completely surprised either; what crimes did they commit?" The fact of Black men being imprisoned is part of the known world, the common sense of known things, normalized to the point of invisibility—you didn't know that; indeed, you didn't even *notice* that. So in another sense, you did know that.

Herman Melville, in his novella *Benito Cereno*, offers a tale that depicts what white folks didn't notice during the rule of slavery. A New England sealing ship operating off the coast of Chile in 1805 comes upon a Spanish frigate drifting aimlessly with tattered sails and a distressed crew, and a figurehead oddly shrouded in canvas bearing the painted slogan: "Follow Your Leader." A small party led by Captain Amasa Delano boards the ship in order to assess the situation and offer help if possible. There they encounter a skeleton crew and a diminished cargo of slaves as well as Captain Benito Cereno, who explains the troubles that had brought them to this point: terrible storms, ill fate and bad luck, disease and fevers that had taken the lives of several, including the slave master Alexandro Aranda.

Captain Delano spends hours aboard ship talking with Benito Cereno, who is always in the company of his loyal slave and servant, Babo. Delano observes and notes a series of strange events—urgent whispering among crew and cargo, a few Africans carrying knives, and an occasional physical confrontation with Spanish crew members. Benito Cereno is pale and weak, often near fainting, always insisting that Babo stay close. As Delano prepares to return to his own ship, a desperate Benito Cereno leaps from the deck onto the departing long boat and the truth becomes clear: Babo is running the ship and Benito Cereno is his prisoner; insurgents have taken control and are demanding a return to Africa; the shrouded figurehead is the bones of Alexandro Aranda, the painted slogan a targeted threat to the crew.

The entire day had been a complex dramatic performance put on by the Africans under the directorial brilliance of Babo to deceive the visitors; in order to see the reality of the drama produced on his behalf—which is bursting with hints and clues and full-blown illumination—Captain Delano, a good liberal Republican from New England, would have needed the one quality he lacked: a deep belief that Babo and the other enslaved cargo were actual people like himself, full human beings capable of intricate planning, complex intelligence, wild imaginations, and historical memory, as well as an acute sense of their own agency.

This is the exact quality we must nourish and grow within ourselves: the ability to open our eyes and see the world and all of humanity in its fullness. People in prison are not things or inferior beings or objects; they too are capable of intricate planning, complex intelligence, wild imaginations, historical memory, and an acute sense of their own agency. The Prison Nation is an intolerable abomination the moment you see that light; joining the insurgency becomes an urgent necessity.

The logic of prison abolition was explained to me by the great freedom fighter Angela Davis: It's a problem of limiting our imaginations, she said, of shutting down our capacity to think more broadly and more bravely. We need to think about what lies beyond prison, beyond making a better or more functional prison system—the focus of too many reform conversations— and initiate massive conversations about de-carceration, that is, bringing folks home and shutting prisons down. Mass incarceration is, after all, part of the afterlife of slavery, and prison abolition is the next step in that long historic project called abolition. As we imagine dramatic change, we should also anticipate future attempts to contain and control, for just as Jim Crow followed abolition, and mass incarceration followed Jim Crow, some evil expression of white supremacy and Black containment as yet unseen lurks just around the corner.

Angela Davis talked about the abolitionist and humane values of liberation, community, restoration, and shared fate as opposed to the hardening practices of cruelty and punishment, revenge and retribution. She reminded us of the ten glorious words uttered by Justice Harry Blackmun in 1994 when he announced publicly that he had become a death penalty abolitionist: "I no longer shall tinker with the machinery of death." He wasn't searching for ways to make state-sanctioned murder more efficient or more palatable— he wanted to get out of the death business altogether. Let's get out of the caging business, she said. Let's not tinker with the machinery of mass incarceration.

I first proposed prison abolition publicly in a talk I gave about Freedom Schools at the University of Pittsburgh. Most of my talk was well received—even when I pointed out, as I always do, that the existence of an American gulag or the Prison Nation meant that you were never far from a prison—but there was a general sense of disbelief when I said I thought prisons should be abolished. The first question from the floor was a request to clarify the point, which I did, saying I thought we should work toward closing all the prisons since they were institutions of congealed violence. The next student up worried that I was kidding—and I assured them I was not—and followed up by politely accusing me of utopian romanticism and unrealistic idealism. Guilty, I said, of the idealism, but not of being unrealistic. The next person tried to show me the error of my logic, and painted a terrifying picture of a world ruled by mass murderers (hmm, I thought), pointing specifically to John Wayne Gacy, the gruesome Chicago serial killer who was the first person executed when Illinois reinstated the death penalty, a person about whom my interrogator had seemingly encyclopedic knowledge. I'm convinced, I said after an exhaustive portrayal, I give up! Okay, that's one cell, I said, so who else? I'll give you Henry Kissinger and Dick Cheney too so now we have three prison cells total—a far cry from the millions we support in reality.

This led to a discussion I've now had countless times with students and others, and it begins with an exercise in the form of a question: Can we—right now—generate a thousand alternatives to caging people? It turns out we can, and so let's.

A Thousand Steps toward De-carceration and a Range of Alternatives to Caging Human Beings (a Start)

1. Decriminalize illegal drugs and expand drug treatment centers to meet the real needs of people caught in the grip of addiction.
2. Use a public health frame to rethink issues of violence.
3. Get guns off the streets.
4. Generously create and support community mental health programs.
5. Build "Community Restorative Justice" projects — spaces where perpetrators and victims can meet with peers and neighbors, community organizers and social workers, to discuss how to repair the harm inflicted by misbehavior.
6. Redirect all misdemeanor offenses away from criminal court with its attendant culture of cruelty, humiliation, and punishment toward counseling, rehab, or anger management for some, and technological support (a simple breathalyzer device, for example, attached to a vehicle before it can be driven) for others.
7. Outlaw all profiteering from prison: ban private prisons, cash bail and bail bond businesses, paid alternatives to jail, the gouging of prisoners by telephone companies, and the privatizing and outsourcing of prison services like clothing and meals.

8. Do away with mandatory minimum sentencing, "three strikes you're out," sentence enhancements, and other punitive measures that serve to swell the prison population.

9. Restore or create opportunities to reduce time inside with policies like day-for-day good time practices.

10. Create massive public works programs.

11. Offer homes to the homeless.

12. Increase the minimum wage to $25 an hour.

13. Grant income supports to the unemployed.

14. Bring the endowments of all private schools, colleges, and universities under public and democratic control, and organize the redistribution of those resources toward a system of free quality education for all.

15. Provide a living-wage stipend, free housing, and good child care to anyone living at or below the poverty line and attending high school or community college.

16. Create a system of free universal health care.

17. Immediately release all prisoners over, say, age fifty for starters.

18. Develop a prisoner's cooperative to operate the institutions, making decisions collectively about all matters concerning food, health care, education, and social services, the organization of work and leisure, and relations with outside institutions including religious, educational, and business organizations.

Whew!

Well, it's a running start. We only have 982 to go! And, yes, none of this is possible in the absence of collective action and a social movement for radical transformation. But we need to work collectively on a vision as part of the fight for abolition. And, yes, some of it may sound a bit like fiddling with the machinery of caging, but let's not be dogmatic hard-liners when actual people could breathe more freely with just a bit of tinkering.

The importance of beginning to make a list is that it shifts the starting point and changes the frame: instead of the ironclad logic of *misbehavior = punishment* and *punishment = prison*, which leads onward and onward without end, we begin to see incarceration as the last and least worthy alternative before us. Think of prison as the one-thousand-and-first option—the last resort and not the only choice. We begin to frame the problem in different terms: recovery and restoration, forgiveness and redemption, public health and human rights, respect and faith.

Alternatives liberate all of us from our own culturally imposed mental prisons, our dimmed consciousness and constrained imaginations. Without alternative ways of thinking and being we become destined to be confined in a lockup state of mind.

Perhaps because we've lived so long in a culture of discipline and punish, or perhaps because the traditional Puritanism became ravenous once again and demanded to be fed, or perhaps because our go-to-jail complex developed obsessive-compulsive disorder linked to attention-deficit hyperactivity—whatever the reasons, many folks hardly noticed as we slipped down the proverbial slope that Angela Davis and Ruthie Gilmore, Erica Meiners, Bernardine Dohrn, Beth Richie, and Dylan Rodriguez had predicted, and we woke up living in a full-blown prison nation. And that fact points to the true and deep-seated reason underneath the phenomenon of mass incarceration: white supremacy dressed up in modern garb, structural racism pure and simple. The system has been dubbed "the new Jim Crow" by the brilliant lawyer and activist Michelle Alexander who points out that there are now more Black men in prison or on probation or parole than there were living in bondage as chattel slaves in 1850; that there are significantly more people caught up in the system of incarceration and supervision in America today—over six million folks—than inhabited Stalin's gulag at its height; that the American gulag constitutes the second largest city in this country, and that while the United States constitutes less than 5 percent of the world's people, it holds over 25 percent of the world's combined prison population; that in the past twenty years the amount states have spent on prisons has risen to six times the rate spent on higher education; and that on any given day tens of thousands of men, overwhelmingly Black and Latino men, are held in the torturous condition known as solitary confinement. You get the picture.

Just as slavery was a defining fact of American life in the nineteenth century, mass incarceration is a central feature in the United States today. And just as the abolition of slavery was unimaginable to most Americans then, a society with no prisons is difficult for people to wrap their heads around now. But try it—imagine a world without prisons.

When enough of us become liberated from the dogma of incarceration and the totalizing logic of captivity and control, we might mobilize ourselves to dive into the hard work of building a political movement to empty the prisons and shut them down. We may look back—just as we look back at slavery—with astonishment and anguish as we realize that the prison-industrial complex was a bad choice: it generated superprofits for a few while it vitalized white supremacy, ruined millions of human lives, devastated social capital, destroyed whole communities, and diminished our society. Slavery, "the peculiar institution," made cruelty customary and unkindness conventional, everyone forced to witness and embrace it as such, or to shut their eyes tight as communities were made more hard-hearted and hateful. Just as the abolition of slavery liberated enormous energy toward a more generous and compassionate social order, so a world without prisons will create the conditions for a more just and decent community for all.

From slavery to lynching, debt peonage, Black Codes, and Jim Crow; from Jim Crow to redlining and entrapment in crowded ghettos with all the concentrated effects of poverty—crumbling tenements, unemployment, homelessness, health problems, inadequate public and social services, crummy schools; from the slums to mass incarceration—the journey is consistent and consistently cruel and inhumane.

✳ ✳ ✳

Now a treacherous conduit has been laid down by the powerful for the children of formerly enslaved human beings, recent immigrants, First Nations people, and the poor—a passage that's earned the colorful metaphoric title "the school-to-prison pipeline." We all know that a pipeline runs in a single direction, and once entered, destiny sweeps everything before it to the bottom. A pipeline offers no exits, no deviations or departures, no way out—unless it fractures. Let's not focus on prison reform or tinkering with the mechanisms of the pipeline to make it "fairer" or more efficient; let's aim, rather, at ripping open the pipeline, upending the assumptions that got us where we are, and then throwing every section of pipe and all the braces and supports into the dustbin of history.

Schools for the poor—many urban and rural schools, and increasingly suburban schools as well—share striking similarities with prisons. In each site discipline and security take precedence over knowledge or human development; in each site people are subordinated to the will of—and forced to follow a strict routine set by—others, isolated from the larger community, and coerced to do work that they have no part in defining; in each folks are regulated and ordered about, indoctrinated and assessed and corrected. Schools for the poor are the prep schools for the prisoners of tomorrow.

To imagine a world without prisons—to become a prison abolitionist—is to join a growing social justice initiative already in motion. It's to join with millions who are thinking of prisons as sites of resistance—places to fight for educational programs, decent health care, and pay for work above slave wages—and whole communities as places of potential radical transformation. It's to link eliminating prisons to revitalizing failing schools, ending homelessness, repairing our broken health care system, overcoming underemployment and unemployment, and ending an economic system based on predation and exploitation. It's to join hands and reclaim and complete the mission of abolition—human liberation and exuberant democracy.

Three

Economic Complex Index

Percent of Swedish workers in trade unions (2013): 67.7

Percent of US workers in trade unions (2013): 10.8

Percent of unionized private-sector US workers in 1900/2015: 6.7/6.7

Hours American workers work (as a percentage) compared to their UK, Norwegian, and Dutch counterparts (2013): + 7, +27, +30

Rank of US in terms of income per hour worked in manufacturing (2010): 11

Number of countries whose GDP is less than the combined fortunes of the five wealthiest Americans (2013): At least 149

Ratio of net worth of the wealthiest 400 Americans to the 150 million poorest Americans (2009): 1/1

Percent change in Wall Street profits from 2007 to 2009: +720

Percent change in unemployment rate from 2007 to 2009: +102

Percent change in total home equity from 2006 to 2009: –61

In contemporary America, belief in the free market economy above all else is absolute. It is unarguable. And yet there is no such thing as a "free market," despite the noisy claims of the fundamentalist marketeers, their apologists in the bought media, and the well-mannered barbarians from the business schools. The "free market" is highly contested, politically managed, extensively regulated, and supported by government policy and our tax dollars at every level — often, but not always, to the advantage of the rich. Historically the free marketeers have howled at the elimination of child labor ("Let the little tykes earn a buck!"), inspections at meatpacking plants, the organizing of trade unions ("Selfish Bolsheviks!"), environmental regulations, clean air and water standards ("The market will sort it all out in the long run"), health and safety regulations in mines and fields and factories, the eight-hour day ("How dare you arrogant elitists deprive the laborer of his freedom to work as many hours as he likes?"), and the abolition of their right to trade in human beings. Of course chattel slavery was but one form of human trade and trafficking, and wage slavery—though different—is another. Today a defining stance of the marketeers is roaming the world in the company of extravagant military power in search of resources and markets as well as dirt-cheap, superexploited labor that can be had without those pesky rules ("Child labor has the added benefit of teaching the natives discipline and obedience right from the start") and then get cast aside without consequence.

More recently the marketeers have found themselves in a bit of a contradiction. The near collapse of the US banking system in 2008 led to George W. Bush nationalizing Fannie Mae and Freddie Mac, the giant mortgage lenders. He instituted one of the biggest state interventions in world history by buying up "toxic assets" to the tune of $700 billion in taxpayer subsidies, and shifting a huge chunk of the financial sector to state ownership. It was a perfect 180-degree pivot: suddenly the market was no longer without fault, and the government no longer broke. In fact the government was now the ideal instrument—streamlined, efficient, and prosperous—to save the day. Bush argued that while the "free market" was still wondrous beyond compare, it nonetheless rested "on the conviction that the . . . government should interfere . . . when necessary." Bush and his fellow racketeers had determined that this was just such a time. Socialism for the rich and the powerful, and capitalist-fabricated dirt and destitution for the rest.

Modern economists extol the wisdom of the "free market" in hushed tones typically reserved for glorifying a holy book, or they mumble about the "laws of the marketplace" as if explaining the laws of magnetism or optics or aerodynamics. When my oldest son was in college, he took Economics

101 and within a couple of weeks he'd figured it out: if you substituted the word "capitalism" every time the textbooks or the professor said "market," "economics," or "industrialism" it made the readings and lectures completely sensible. Economics was simply a metric that reflected political choices and (with more or less accuracy) the social and class relations of society. When he asked why the course wasn't called Capitalism 101, the professor responded, "Same thing." Indeed.

Economists quantify everything, disguising their values and their meanings in a mystifying faux language of objectivity. They advise the rest of us ordinary folks, as the Wizard advised the four seekers in the throne room in Oz, "Pay no attention to that man behind the curtain."

Let's look anyway.

It would be more honest to admit that economics—like history or anthropology or political science—is a smashing together of the subjective and the objective, or, more precisely an *interpretive* look at facts and forces that exist in the world. It's the gathering of statistics in order to describe and construct the world, and the decision as to what we count is of primary importance. Neither the facts and forces nor the interpretations are beyond the comprehension of us mere mortals. We don't need to be technical experts to be active citizens engaged in the big questions that impact who we are or what we become as people or as a society. We can know we want clean food and water without being epidemiologists; we can say that we want bridges to hold up and airplanes to stay in the air without degrees in engineering; we can recognize that gross disparities in wealth distort and destroy democracy without spreadsheets that can only be read with a magnifying glass; we can decide that nuclear power plants are a bad idea without PhDs in physics. And we can decide we want a system of production and distribution that is transparent, participatory, and in the service of the general welfare—it's not rocket science. Oh, and we can decide what kinds of rockets ought to be built too and how they should be used.

All the rules of the economy are made up and put in place by people, and they can't really exist beyond or outside of human culture and politics. Anything made by people can be unmade or remade by people. While there is surely a real world of hard edges and data points, it's not a world beyond the basic human enterprise of meaning-making, nor is it a world beyond values and ethics and political calculation. The economic system is not beyond our capacity to alter or even abolish it. Even a brief glance at history reminds us of our often astonishing power to correct or amend or, if we choose, to revolutionize all that we see before us. This is where a vital and robust public—and a mobilized social upheaval when necessary—makes all the difference.

If we pay attention we can see before our eyes the consequences of economic laws that are conjured from thin air. In response to the quite real threat of cataclysmic climate change, for example, some governments have agreed to "marketize" carbon—to make carbon pollution something to bank up, buy, and sell at a spanking-new marketplace. "Cap and trade" programs across Europe haven't slowed CO_2 emissions an iota, but they have spawned a multibillion-dollar commodities market trading carbon credits for profit. We might have chosen, with fierce and sustained opposition from the filthy extractors and the deadly destroyers no doubt, to ban polluting activities altogether, to prioritize wind and solar energy, or to create tougher regulations, but the fundamentalists prevailed, inventing a whole range of new categories and rules, and —*presto*— carbon is suddenly a part of the "natural" logic of the market, which is nothing more than a newfangled casino with poison as its currency.

The Chicago Public Schools (CPS) recently adopted Pay for Success, a program funded with so-called social impact bonds, a partnership between investors and corporate philanthropies designed as a profit-making venture in the public sector. Pay for Success was used in Utah to prevent 99 percent of children supposedly headed for special education from actually being identified for those programs, and paid the giant Wall Street firm Goldman Sachs and other investors for each child *not* placed in special education. When the first cohort of students under the program enters kindergarten, CPS will begin paying lenders for each *fewer* child assigned to special education when compared to a control group— Goldman Sachs will receive more than $9,000 every year for each identified child who does *not* receive special education. What evil genius thought that up?

Michigan governor Rick Snyder took office in 2011 vowing to run the state like a business. Snyder had amassed a fortune as a venture capitalist, and he pledged to deploy his super-slick business skills and experiences as governor. He moved quickly to cut business taxes as well as taxes on the rich, and he aggressively pushed and passed anti-union legislation. He also signed a controversial bill into law that allowed the state to install powerful emergency managers in municipalities in order to take control of all local financial matters, supposedly in the interest of curbing spending and balancing budgets. Today more than half of Michigan's Black population lives in cities where the local government—appointed not elected—is being run like a business.

The results are in, notably in Flint where the unelected manager chose to switch the source of municipal water from the Detroit River to the toxic Flint River, saving money but at the same time poisoning the residents. Capitalism at work! Thousands of children suffered elevated lead levels, and the health impacts on the entire population have been catastrophic as well, but that's capitalism. It's worth noting that the determined and sustained activism of the people of Flint themselves in the face of official denial and cover-up has been exemplary—without action from below the pain and suffering would have remained local and hidden, and no remedies would be in sight. In the face of escalating lawsuits and demands for accountability, Snyder appropriated a million dollars of state money for his own legal fees.

But now we see clearly that *everything* is quantified and *everything* has its price under capitalism. Everything can be bought and sold; everything is reduced to a cash nexus. Birthing a child, cancer treatments, childhood vaccinations, clean water—everything is monetized. We're encouraged to know the *price* of everything but the *value* of nothing. We're instructed to think of health, for example, not as a human right or a common good, but as an industry—the health care industry. Similarly it becomes less and less jarring to hear talk of the housing market (as opposed to housing), the food industry (not food as an obvious universal need), and the public safety and education markets. The water bazaar is well under way; still to come: the air exchange. This is the way it is, but this is not the way it has to be—not at all.

Labor, of course, is a source of pride and satisfaction as well as the root of all social wealth, an honorable and ethical activity when it helps workers and the wider community. Human beings from the start long for work that is real. But when labor is alienated, when the worker is estranged from the created product or service, when work exploits, oppresses, harms, destroys, kills, and degrades people or our shared world, it becomes corrupted. In a predatory system the noble nature of labor is amended, and work becomes a necessary evil. When work is recast as a bummer involving only the sacrifice of leisure and comfort, the worker becomes more resistant to labor. But because work is necessary, the worker fights to maximize wages and compensation.

The boss faces the same conflict and contradiction in that little con game, but from the other side: the owner of the means of production has in mind an ideal end point of limitless production, expansion, and profit without workers constantly demanding things like food and rest and shelter. To the owner, labor is nothing but a cost of production, and so the boss fights relentlessly to reduce that cost in every imaginable way—dividing labor into smaller and smaller unskilled bits, plundering resources and human bodies, promoting white and male supremacy, speeding up production lines, introducing automation and implementing technological advances, suppressing wages by destroying trade unions and work rules, shuttering whole industries and relocating to impoverished nations where labor is cheap and regulations nonexistent, trafficking in human beings as semi-slaves, and even exploiting the labor of children. The boss dreams and schemes to eliminate workers altogether while maximizing and expanding wealth.

There is little or no consideration for the greater good in this approach beyond a kind of orthodoxy that the market is natural, inevitable, and entirely wise—and that it exists, therefore, automatically for the greater good. This is entirely fact-free and faith-based dogma, but it's trotted out on every occasion to dress up in colorful clothing the relentless drive for cheap resources and cheap labor, maximum profit and minimum cost. Automobiles and oil and highways are made to seem normal and rational as the chief means of moving from place to place—without any alternative whatsoever. But if the opening question were a consideration of the best types of transportation, various forms that fit the needs of people and do minimum harm to the earth, an imaginative world opens up, and we begin to see lots and lots of alternatives. Technological innovations would be worthy, then—redirected away from producing superprofits for a few and superexploited labor for the many, and toward meeting people's needs while eliminating exploitation and galloping consumerism altogether.

A modest use of resources is preferable to an excessive use since resources are *everywhere* limited, and as E. F. Schumacher, the British economist, argues in his classic little book *Small Is Beautiful*, "People who live in highly self-sufficient local communities are less likely to get involved in large-scale violence than people whose existence depends on worldwide systems of trade."[1] We might advocate, then, never taking a ride—even on public transportation—if one can walk or ride a bike instead. We are now explicitly speaking in a different register: values, ethics, politics, human purposes, and real choice.

Activists in Detroit today are engaged in an ongoing effort to "reimagine, reculture, and rebuild" our dying cities. They are promoting a revolution in values and a reformation on the ground: urban farming, cooperative bakeries, housing rehabilitation, alternative people-centered transportation (in the Motor City!), collective art projects, occupying and taking over schools and health clinics in order to serve the people. Their slogans are intentionally provocative: "Detroit: City of Hope," "Detroit Is All of Us," "Detroit Is the Future." They are signaling that the crisis of capitalist deindustrialization is not unique to Detroit, and that when we work toward solutions we should reject the path of investments in casinos or prisons in favor of deeper and more humane transformations that can only be found when we mobilize people power.

✳ ✳ ✳

Thinking in radically different ways about *work* and *want*,
productivity and human *need* creates a sturdier ground from
which to challenge all manner of conventional thinking: government is broke; we can't as a society create public work
projects or build a free universal health care system or guarantee incomes for older people; because people have been
living lavishly and beyond their means for decades, workers
must labor much longer and retire with much less; policies
that help wealthy people get richer will have a "trickle-down"
benefit that will magically make all the rest of us better off;
heavily taxing the rich is both unfair and suppresses economic growth; the "invisible hand of the market" is the secret
sauce that brings prosperity and happiness to all; and what's
good for Wall Street is good for America. All of this accepted
wisdom is just a collection of clichés—nothing more than
gobbledygook and pure bullshit.

Take the question of support for older people. Cuts in
benefits to the elderly—disguised as increases in minimum
retirement ages, or the ages at which full pension or retirement benefits can be realized—are idiotic on their own terms.
They're based on a popularly promoted bit of common sense:
we are living longer, there are fewer workers to support the
elderly, and we must therefore work longer and get less. This
perversely powerful logic is completely erroneous.

It turns out upon closer examination that "we" are not
actually living longer: wealthy people are living longer; non-
wealthy people, not so much. It's been widely reported that

middle-aged white men are now dying in unprecedented numbers from suicide, alcoholism, and drug overdoses—another signal of a social system on the edge. "Raising the retirement age cuts benefits for those who can't wait to retire and who often won't live long," James K. Galbraith argues. "Meanwhile, richer people with soft jobs work on." Furthermore, a lot of workers retire because they can't find jobs: "Extending the retirement age for them just means a longer job search, a futile waste of time and effort."[2]

Frankly we don't need another factory or workplace staffed by old folks to make another line of widgets, nor do we need more workers to produce the goods we actually consume. We certainly don't need more casinos and more prisons—well, the powerful may in order to crush and control, but we, the people, do not—or more war spending as the last and most desperate attempt at a massive jobs program. One of the truly profound problems we face is finding a way to separate "jobs" from meaningful, useful, and fulfilling work for all—work that promotes the common good and the welfare of the community, work that enhances the human sense of purpose and productivity.

Work is surely a source of satisfaction—it allows us to take care of ourselves and our families, for starters. But work can also promote feelings of pride and purpose at a sheet of metal cut properly or a difficult weld executed correctly or a deadline met or a problem solved creatively in a coordinated team effort—even though the fruits of our labor, the profit, is typically taken, alienating us from our work in some fundamental sense. And there's a lot of important work to be done—taking care of the very young and the disabled and the elderly, fixing the roads and the bridges and the water systems, improving housing, growing healthy food, reinventing transport—but these things don't always translate neatly or easily into the profit-oriented "jobs economy," and that's the problem of labor in ethical terms. We all need work; we all want to find meaning and happiness in our labor. Some work can give us great satisfaction but does not provide a proper income, while some jobs can offer us a wage—drone operator, prison guard, sniper—but cross a line into a shameful territory where pride becomes perverse.

The primary and essential labor of human beings is what Ai-jen Poo and the courageous women who organize as Domestic Workers United call "the work of caring and helping." Poo and her colleagues organize a workforce that is largely immigrant women of color, mostly marginalized and super-exploited, and they realize that class identity is fundamentally formed in solidarity and struggle—it's not automatic. They rethink labor, invoking images of mothering and parenting, teaching and caregiving, gardening and repairing. They imagine radically different relationships and argue that the real business of people and the real work of the world is not building "the economy" but is, in fact, building one another as living human beings of mutual creation. At the same time, these sisters want to be treated fairly as workers with adequate compensation, good benefits, and basic rights.

There are many other vivid examples and models of human cooperation, union and community building, and the co-creation of one another and our shared world. In the Basque Country of Spain, worker-owned and -managed enterprises have multiplied over decades as workers have come together in the spirit of economic democracy and justice to build viable alternatives to corporate power and predation. The co-op movement in general, and the associations under the umbrella called Mondragon in particular, call explicitly for the construction of a freer, fairer, and more caring Basque society through economic and social reconstruction. The organization rests on principles of sufficient and fair pay, basic equality of worker-members—"their rights to be, possess, and know"—transparency, enduring universal education, full participation of all in the democratic process and the sovereignty of an elected General Assembly.

Immigrant women created a women-owned, eco-friendly house-cleaning business in Brooklyn, New York—Si Se Puede! Women's Cooperative provides social supports and educational opportunities for its members and creates living-wage jobs that are performed in safe and healthy environments. In the Bronx the Cooperative Home Care Associates, a worker-owned home care agency, offers quality home care to clients and decent jobs for direct-care workers. Started with twelve home health aides in 1995 it now employs more than twenty-five hundred people and delivers free training for six hundred low-income and unemployed women annually.

When workers at Republic Windows and Doors in Chicago noticed large pieces of equipment being removed from the Goose Island warehouse in 2008, they suspected that a closing was imminent; when they learned that the owners had purchased Echo Windows and Doors, a nonunion shop in Red Oak, Iowa, the writing was on the wall. Maintenance worker and local president Armando Robles and his team began mapping contingencies, and when the bosses announced that operations would cease, 260 workers would be laid off without receiving accrued sick or vacation days, and their health insurance would be immediately terminated, 200 workers took control of the plant, moved in, and barricaded the place. Progressive churches, communities, and other unions mobilized in support, and within a week the workers had won their demands for fair compensation and continued health coverage.

That's just the start of the story, according to James Thindwa, a dazzling and effective community organizer and strategist in Chicago via Zimbabwe, Malawi, and Miami University who was active throughout. Thindwa's family had taken part in Rhodesia's fight against British colonial rule, and as a youngster he had absorbed a profound lesson about the power of organized labor and mass protest: "Unions to us, growing up, performed more functions than just negotiating for better wages for workers. They really were seen . . . as a legitimate vehicle for transforming society." As the workers at Republic learned the same lesson, Thindwa told me that the takeover demonstrated concretely where real power and wisdom resides, and before long the workers decided to manage their own collective destiny as owner-operators at Republic. "That's a vital model for others to learn from," he said.

* * *

People are fighting back in every corner and from every vantage point: Occupy Wall Street! Occupy the Farm! Occupy the Hood! Occupy the Pentagon! Seize the State House! Occupy Hong Kong and Istanbul! On and on and on: occupy the schools and the community health clinics, occupy the media and your imagination, occupy as metaphor—a free space where every grievance is welcome and every hope is grounded and embodied. Of course, Occupy Wall Street did not end the predatory financial system, overthrow zombie capitalism, or smash the state, but those are pretty high bars, and only a cynic would cite those as movement failures. Occupy did accomplish a significant reframing of the national conversation about income inequality, poverty, and exploitation; it introduced the wildly imaginative metaphor of the 1 percent and the 99 percent; it made the taxes paid by the wealthy an object of scrutiny and critique. Before Occupy happened, all of that was dreamy and impossible; after it happened it looked as if it had been inevitable all along.

In 2015, young Black people dramatically reframed the serial killing of Black youth, naming, documenting, exposing, and challenging state violence: the visible and undeniable militarized police occupation of Black communities, the impunity with which police murder Black young (and not so young) people, and the institutionalized white supremacy embodied in the carceral police state. Black Lives Matter exploded into public consciousness as a radical, national social movement. Again, cynics may say that the movement hasn't obliterated the racist system—true—but it has indeed upended the consciousness of millions, changed the frame on the role of the police in a democracy, for example, the place of prisons, what Black liberation could and should look like, and the kind of society we need to build if we are to gain a humane future.

Who knows where the next explosion of resistance will burst forth, and who can say how far it will take us toward liberation? Contradictions between the workers and the bosses, the haves and the have-nots, the 1 percent and the 99 percent, are intensifying daily, and our worldwide interconnectedness is more tangled, complex, durable, and fragile day by day. Who can predict with any certainty which specific spark of the millions relentlessly flaring up and dying down will ignite a global uprising? A land seizure by First Nations people in California or by peasants and farmers in India; a walkout by factory workers in China; a village takeover in Mexico or the capture of a manufacturing plant in Brazil; a mobilization of the homeless in Detroit or New Orleans to control and rebuild sections of their abandoned cities or of youth in Cleveland and Oakland to disarm the cops; a mass jailbreak with community support and coordination or the transformation of a corporation into a worker-owned co-op— each of these and more is already happening; each carries the potential to bring down the old and usher in the new. A single spark can start a prairie fire.

✳ ✳ ✳

Of course we live in the era of late global capitalism, and the ways in which production is organized and developed impacts our values and attitudes and perceptions—indeed, not only our way of life but our whole conception of reality and possibility. When James Carville, candidate Bill Clinton's campaign manager, rallied and focused his troops with his now-famous reminder, "It's the economy, stupid!" he was echoing a view that is widely shared today: Materialism—the forces and relations of production, owned, organized, and managed by the rich and powerful—is the driving force of human history.

In perhaps the most elegant and extravagant praise-song ever written about capitalism—exceeding in both style and rapture anything from the pen of Ayn Rand or the mouths of Alan Greenspan or Donald Trump—one of capitalism's greatest admirers claims that in scarcely a hundred years, capitalists "created more massive and more colossal productive forces than have all preceding generations together. Subjugation of nature's forces to man, machinery, application of chemistry to industry and agriculture, steam navigation, railways . . . clearing of whole continents for cultivation, canalization of rivers, whole populations conjured out of the ground." Capitalism's actions and activities are awe-inspiring and breathtaking to behold: "It has accomplished wonders far surpassing Egyptian pyramids, Roman aqueducts, and Gothic cathedrals; it has conducted expeditions that put in the shade all former Exoduses of nations and crusades." This is Karl Marx and Friedrich Engels at their exuberant best.

It's often assumed that the *Communist Manifesto*, first issued in 1848, is a diatribe against capitalism, or a handbook for taking power and installing a communist dictatorship, but it's not true. The *Manifesto* identifies capitalism as a historic artifact to be examined and understood, something that was born in certain conditions, is driven by certain laws, and will, like everything else, one day die—this is in the first place a brief explanation of the materialist conception of history, or the ways in which the organization of production drives human affairs: "It's the economy, stupid!"

But the major contribution of the little book surprises many people who actually take the time to read it: Marx and Engels practically swoon at capitalism's protean nature, its inherent and permanent *revolutionary* character, and its unprecedented accomplishments: "The bourgeoisie cannot exist without constantly revolutionizing the instruments of production, and thereby the relations of production, and with them the whole relations of society," they rejoice. "All fixed, fast-frozen relations, with their train of ancient and venerable prejudices and opinions, are swept away, all newly formed ones become antiquated before they can ossify. All that is solid melts into air, all which is holy is profaned, and man is at last compelled to face with sober senses, his real conditions of life, and his relations with his kind." Capitalism is the most dynamic economic system ever known, a giant swirling vortex sweeping aside all in its path in its incessant drive for profit and new production, and Marx and Engels are swept away as well.

Their admiration for capitalism extends to its scope and range, its world horizon and its cosmopolitanism. The industrial revolution broke open and overwhelmed all existing borders, and the constant quest for raw materials, cheap labor, and new markets "chases the bourgeoisie over the whole surface of the globe." Here they anticipate globalization, a buzzword of contemporary life: "In place of the old local and national seclusion and self-sufficiency, we have intercourse in every direction, universal interdependence of nations. And as in the material, so also in the intellectual/spiritual production. . . . National one-sidedness and narrow-mindedness become more and more impossible, and from the numerous national and local literatures, there arises a world literature." We might say a global culture, in every sphere. The achievement of a world horizon was a wonder and the foundation for imagining and then creating a future society.

Their awe and admiration do not, however, blunt the searing condemnation of capitalist exploitation and immiseration or their withering critique of its injustices, built-in oppressiveness, and incorrigible avariciousness. Their most intense and insightful indictment is reserved for what capitalism does to our humanity, the fundamental degradation and perversion of our humanness. Capitalism reduces people to objects, things to be used, numbered, labeled, conscripted, and coordinated; it brings to prominence our basest qualities, greed and fear, and necessarily forces people to subordinate and suppress our natural sense of cooperation and kinship in order to survive in a cold, harsh world. Capitalism "has left remaining no other nexus between man and man than naked self-interest, than callous 'cash payment'"; it has essentially reduced every norm of freedom "into that single, unconscionable freedom—free trade." "Money is the universal, self-constituted value of all things," they write. "It has therefore robbed the whole world, human as well as natural, of its own values. Money is the alienated essence of man's work and being. This alien essence dominates him and he adores it."

What kinds of people do we want to become? Can we imagine advancing beyond the predatory phase in human affairs, envisioning a place of more, not less, participatory democracy, more, not less, economic justice, more respect for civil liberties and more tolerance for private lives, more public culture and more joyous shared space, more peace and dialogue and disarmament and camaraderie and fellowship and sisterhood and solidarity and reconciliation? Can we find avenues to participate now in efforts to create and support worker-owned enterprises, cooperatives, collectives, and unions through negotiation where possible and occupations, seizures, and takeovers where necessary? Can we mobilize a messy, raucous, and lengthy community meeting where everyone learns to make something (vegetable stir-fry, tortillas, lentil soup, pasta salad) from scratch, avoids looking at a clock or a screen, and considers how much stuff is too much stuff?

Imagine the burden and the satisfaction of engaging in whatever we collectively deem to be the common good; imagine focusing our attention and weighing in about issues that often seem distant or obscure or somehow best handled by the experts: food production and distribution, child and elder care, education, housing, justice, community health, infrastructure development, neighborhood gardens and parks and murals. Imagine what it would mean to have voluntary and universal community service, say at eighteen, everyone choosing to devote a year of service in one of ten areas determined of, by, and for the people—we'd likely have more powerful investments and opinions and political priorities about who we are and what we want to become. And then imagine keeping it growing: a year of voluntary service at twenty-eight, thirty-eight, forty-eight, and fifty-eight. We'd all be better for it, and it might help us collectively create a vibrant, robust, and authentically participatory democracy.

What does it mean to be human today?

How shall we live?

Imagining the future society we would like for future generations, we unleash our spiritual and social imaginations. We think of children and grandchildren, and of grandchildren's grandchildren precisely because a co-invented and dramatically extended family, at its evolving best, can be a small-scale model of a mini-society driven by norms of equality and reciprocity, a sense of shared community in which people care about and for one another, mutual respect, recognition of differences including distinct capacities and interests and needs, shared wealth, attempts to account for and correct all chance/accidental disadvantages, and so on—from each according to what he or she is capable of, and to each according to need.

There it is, the wild but in some sense the universal "family": imperfect to be sure, a little off-kilter and slightly dysfunctional by definition, and yet at its best a model of everyday anarchy and commonsense socialism.

Four

Debt Index

Average amount of student loan debt for all graduating seniors with student loans (2014): $28,950

Average amount of student loan debt for all graduating seniors with student loans (1994): $10,100

Total outstanding student loan debt (May 2013): $1.2 trillion

Household net worth lost during Great Recession: $16.4 trillion

Percentage of inflation-adjusted median wealth lost by African American households (2005–2009): 66

Ratio of white/African American median household net worth, 2005 compared to 2010: 12/1 compared to 22/1

Foreclosure starts (2008–2012): 8,659,644

US credit card debt (January 2016): $935.3 billion

Developing countries' total external debt in current US dollars (2014): $5,393,390,684,031

A couple of years ago I spoke to a group of students at a large public university. My focus was on naming the current political moment, and the talk veered inevitably to student loans and to debt more generally. About ten minutes in, a hefty contingent of Hell's Angels in full regalia and with Tea Party Patriot patches prominently displayed on their arms ambled in and took front-row seats. I paused as they settled in, took a deep breath, and went on.

After forty minutes the floor was open for questions, and first to the microphone was the leader of the Angels. "I'm surprised to tell you that I agreed with most of what you said," he began. "But I worry that you're a tax-and-spend-liberal and a big government guy." I tried to reassure him: I'm no liberal, I began, and I'm no big government guy either. I'm opposed to huge rapacious corporations controlling government, big or small, at every level—which is just what we've got here now. But let's be clear: the function of government is to tax and to spend, period. So the real question we should focus on is not who's a liberal or who's a patriot, but who you want to tax and what and where you want to spend the people's resources, oh, and who decides?

You and your comrades, I continued, rode up here on a highway built with common funds collected from taxes. You might think that was a good thing and money well spent, even if it is a collective project and could be considered a "social-ist road" from one perspective. You crossed over bridges and aqueducts where clean water was being pumped into the city while clean air swirled around you; maybe those collective undertakings are good things too? Make up your own mind, I said, but I want the people—not the big banks and predatory lenders, not the profit-hungry corporations and their bought lawmakers—to decide what's in our common interest. One of my slogans could be, "Tax the rich and build strong bridges." He smiled and nodded slightly.

But, I continued, maybe in the spirit of challenging big government and getting rid of massive waste and towering debt we could agree to close the Pentagon and shut down the military. That would save the United States at least a trillion dollars a year in a single stroke. There was a burst of applause from the students. "Not so fast," he replied. "Not the Penta-gon." So now *you're* the big government person and the guy driving up the deficit, I pointed out. We shared a laugh and later went out to a restaurant and kept talking.

What's a six-syllable word constructed from four other words smashed together that is used by the mouthpieces of unrestrained avariciousness as an epithet hurled at anyone who defies the orthodoxy of predatory capitalism?

Taxandspendliberal (tax-n-spend-LI-bral), *n.* A weak-willed whiner who lacks gumption, opposes tax cuts for the "makers" and the "job creators," supports the "nanny state," and spends most of the time sniveling about being entitled to things like a job and a place to live, food, education, and health care, all the while begging for more government hand-outs for the undeserving poor and more giveaways to the shiftless "takers."

It's such a powerful bludgeon and it rolls so easily off the tongue that right-wing politicians and talking heads simply can't stop saying it: *taxandspendliberal.* They love the sound of it. And the first part of the word, "tax," is itself so toxic in political circles that actual liberals can barely squeak the word out, preferring a range of euphemisms—monies, tariffs, revenues, co-pays, deductibles—as they too call for all manner of tax cuts. It is, however, a fraudulent and hypocritical sleight of hand: the business of government—liberal or conservative, open or authoritarian, feudal, theocratic, royal, capitalist, fascist, autocratic, socialist, or whatever, it makes no difference—is always the business of taxing and spending. Always. And everyone knows it even though no one in the electoral politics game will offer an honest and straightforward argument about it. Ask a conservative US senator to vote for universal health care and you'll be accused of being a taxandspendliberal and a communist agitator to boot as you're driven from his office; ask the same senator to *cut* taxes substantially by closing all US military facilities abroad and ending military aid to Israel, Saudi Arabia, and Egypt and you'll be called a communist again. You can't win with these guys.

People refer to government provisions they tend to favor (veteran's benefits—which are nonetheless stingily meted out—or farm subsidies—which mainly benefit Big Agriculture) as "insurance" for "taxpayers." Government assistance (Medicaid or Aid to Familes with Dependent Children) is disparaged or cast as "welfare" for the lazy "takers." The arguments for and against become a tangle of rationalizations and hypocrisies: one type of aid evens the playing field or gives folks a boost to get on their feet, while the other type encourages a culture of dependency, discourages initiative, and breeds a practice of slothfulness.

If they're honest, liberals and conservatives, reactionaries and radicals alike, as well as people bridging the widest possible political reaches, will agree that some folks ought to be taxed at certain set rates in order to mutually support the things we decide are our collective needs. The US Constitution gives Congress the power "to lay and collect taxes, duties, imports and excises, to pay the debts and provide for the common defense and general welfare." The only questions worth debating are who should be taxed? How much? Who decides? What constitutes the general welfare and what should the collective pool of tax funds be spent on? What would be fair and just? Or, how can we create a society in which each of us contributes what we can to the common good, and each of us receives what we need in order to live in dignity?

✳ ✳ ✳

In 1776 Adam Smith wrote in favor of taxation: "The subjects of every state ought to contribute towards the support of the government, as nearly as possible, in proportion to their respective abilities."[1] Reasonable enough—sounds like something Jesus might have said, or Karl Marx. But during the drafting of the US Constitution, the powerful Southern states wanted enslaved human beings counted as *people* for the purpose of representation only, and definitely not counted as people for the purposes of taxation. Southern slavers wanted a large say in the business of government, but simultaneously wanted a small tax burden—the famous depraved "three-fifths compromise" whereby enslaved workers counted as a bit more than half a person was encoded in the Constitution. The American antitax tradition—like so much of the everyday business in the "Land of the Free"—is rooted in slavery, not liberty or democracy.

In contemporary conversation about taxes, spending, debt, and forgiveness, the American legacy is on full display: "public" is consistently colored in racial terms—public welfare, public housing, public hospital. Language is corrupted in other ways as well—large and small—moving away from conversation and debate about human rights and self-evident truths toward insistent talk of accumulation and profit as the only sensible lens through which to view the world. Discourse becomes degraded as nothing more than a dogmatic recitation of the gospel according to Mammon: the "food industry," as I noted earlier, instead of food; the "housing market," not shelter; the "education business," not teaching and learning; the "health care market" rather than healthy people in strong

and vital communities. Alongside this pervasive phenomenon, citizens are recast as "taxpayers" and "consumers" as if
those were the defining features of our lives, beyond voting or
participation or cooperating in the public square.

Today's privatization—or as it's more fashionably called,
"private-public partnerships"—is essentially transferring productive public goods and assets from the community to private owners who can use those assets as they see fit. These
goods and assets include natural resources like water and forests, and services like fire protection, parks and recreation,
streets and sanitation. They might also include enterprises
that we as a community or a polity decide are in our common interest: schools and universities, hospitals and clinics,
transportation and public safety. All of this is putatively held
in trust by the government for the good of all.

Where we might see a public good, however, the privat-
izers, marketeers, banksters, and their hedge-fund homies see
only pulsating, gleaming, dazzlingly lit dollar signs. Every
public park is a potential shopping mall, every public college
an opportunity to issue predatory, taxpayer-backed student
loans, every Third World nation a potential site of extraction
and super-exploited labor. The sacred becomes profane.
Whenever someone asserts that government engages the private sector to do a great deal of the public business, flip that
script: corporations engage the government whenever they
see an opportunity to make a profit. The private-public partnership boils down to this: private profit, public cost.

Privatization is an iron dogma, faith based and fact free, a
fundamental orthodoxy imposed everywhere. The wonder of

dogma, of course, is that it exists in a world all its own, feeding itself a steady diet of easy belief as comfort food, unencumbered by evidence, argument, reason, or doubt. The fact that privately run, for-profit prisons are demonstrably corrupt and inefficient, and that they, like all capitalist enterprises, are a whirling vortex of accumulation that must expand or die, is swept under the rug. The fact that the private auto industry recently collapsed and capitalist Wall Street drove the economy to ground—and both were bailed out by the public—is of no consequence. The market is a religion, as insistent and intolerant as any other fundamentalism, and its priests are the well-bred barbarians from the business schools assuring the ignorant masses that the market has "wisdom" and operates with a mysterious and "invisible hand" that you will only see if you drink the Kool-Aid and convert. Believe in Mammon and worship at His altar or be cast out and doomed to wander east of Wall Street with the other infidels.

We must mobilize to fight for the democratic right of people to control their own public institutions, resist the fraud of private-public partnerships as well as tax policies that are so grotesquely unfair that Bill Gates, to take but one gleaming example, becomes richer than God, and can appoint himself the de facto high commissioner of US education (as well as global guru of health and agricultural policy) and no one can stop him. Talk about government largesse! Clearly Gates was not taxed enough—those billions of dollars could and should be in the public domain, their disposition subject to the will of the people and not the autocratic and arbitrary whims of Himself alone. Bill Gates said earnestly in 2014 that it was easier to solve the problem of malaria globally than it was to solve the problem of failing schools in the United States; a friend pointed out that in Bill and Melinda Gates's neighborhood there's no malaria and no failing schools: problem solved!

Regressive tax policy degrades democracy as it dresses up the "takers" in clever disguises and transforms them magically into "makers." Bill Gates turns out to have been sucking at the teat of the state all this time, his taking entirely destructive and unaffordable, while he is celebrated widely as a genius and a maker. The Bill and Melinda Gates Foundation with its irritating "mission statement" announcing its belief that every child should have a *chance* to lead a full and productive life—not the right to actually *lead* that life, but merely a *chance* at it—is another tax boondoggle in a long tradition of corporate corruption and fraud.

Carnegie, Rockefeller, Ford, MacArthur, Gates—the names and the "good works" have become so normalized that we hardly notice the deeper intent and the wider impact. Carnegie and Rockefeller exploited their employees, polluted the earth, extracted their wealth from the earth and the bodies of their workers. They then rebranded themselves as generous and beneficent good guys who build libraries. Carnegie should have paid his workers a fair wage, or perhaps his profits should have been taxed enough so that we, the people, could have built public libraries and developed the vaccines without the patronizing hand of charity. Charity, after all, is not social justice. But libraries and vaccines—effective tools in reputation rehabilitation—are merely one benign face of a much larger effort at corporate control of public policy in all areas.

In Illinois, we have a regressive flat-tax where everyone pays the same rate of taxes, which leads to a huge band of millionaires cashing in and taking from the common good: James McNerney Jr., CEO of Boeing, who made $23.3 million in 2010, paid the same rate as an associate at Walmart in Joliet; David Nelms, CEO of Discover Financial Services, made $21.2 million and paid the same rate as a kindergarten teacher in East St. Louis; Thomas Wilson, CEO of Allstate made $16.0 million and paid the same rate as a firefighter in Chicago. Oh, and Boeing, McNerney's racket, received a $30 billion Pentagon contract in 2010 to build 179 airborne tankers and got a $124 million refund from the IRS that same year. Your tax dollars at work!

To round out the picture, corporations steal billions of dollars annually from the public purse by setting up shell companies in Delaware and offshore accounts to front their businesses in the Cayman Islands or Panama, and thereby avoid taxes: an unstaffed office in Dublin can serve as headquarters for a thriving company in Hartford. Boeing has received $58 billion in taxpayer-subsidized loans and guarantees from the Export-Import Bank since 1994 and has eliminated fifty-seven thousand jobs in the United States in that same period as it outsourced and moved capital and resources freely around the globe. Boeing extorts billions from local governments with incessant threats of relocation, and it's not alone: it's estimated that large welfare subsidies for American corporations from city, county, and state governments add up to $80 billion a year, mostly as incentives to operate locally.

There is *no sales tax* on the trading of financial securities—the purchase of stocks, derivatives, and other financial instruments—the total value of which is many times more than the world economy. A homeless person buying one meatball with no spaghetti at the Golden Spike pays more actual taxes—real money—than a market speculator.

Hedge fund managers who profit from shortages of homes and food pay a smaller percentage in taxes than people making thousands of times less, and have the opportunity to *defer all* of their taxes indefinitely. Therefore, superrich stock owners can do nothing except wait for the market to come to them and make up to $10 billion in a year, enough to pay the salaries of half a million teachers. The superrich are not the people who invented the laser or the transistor, nor are they the folks who discovered DNA. They are mostly speculators and coupon-clippers or people who are good at rent-seeking and wealth appropriation, mostly in figuring out how to get a larger share of an existing pie.

Your tax dollars are at work in a tangle of other ways that are lucrative to the takers and the cheaters: the Internet was *started* with public money as the Pentagon's ARPANET; the National Science Foundation funded the Digital Library Initiative research at Stanford University; and a massive geographical database was developed by the US Census Bureau—all three projects, paid for through taxes, have been crucial to the development of Google, which now reaps private superprofits.

Big Pharma—which is a profit-generating machine that doesn't give a shit about anyone's health—has always relied on basic research performed with public funds at the National Institutes of Health; Big Oil rides on public roads and ports and rail; Big Science treats publicly funded discoveries as business secrets to be profitably monetized; Big Banks, which are "too big to fail," reap billions as the capitalist state sets itself up as the lender of last resort and underwrites every risk the Wall Street gang gins up.

There it is: socialism for the rich!

When Willie Sutton, the American bank robber, was asked why he robbed banks, he famously replied, "That's where the money is." Of course it's a blazing truth that robbing banks is the work of petty, two-bit crooks; the thief's deeper dream is to *own* the bank—that's where the real money is.

A smart video emerged from the student-led struggles at the University of California that had been organized to resist the grinding and relentless undoing of public higher education: a camera follows along as a student attends to the daily routine—writing, reading, taking notes at a lecture—while a voiceover offers a steady tabulation of the costs associated with each step: "pen: $1.69; textbook: $38; backpack: $69; dinner (a tiny packet of ramen noodles!): $0.50." At the end of the list: "Education: [pause] . . . Priceless." And then the devastatingly perfect tagline: "There are some things that money can't buy; don't let education be one of them."

The crisis in public higher education is painfully real and entirely fraudulent, manufactured by the banksters: tuition and fees are skyrocketing across the country and are already out of reach for millions; staff cutbacks, layoffs, and reductions in student services are now commonplace; massive student loans are replacing grants and scholarships; class size is increasing while course offerings are decreasing; hiring freezes and pay cuts and unpaid mandatory furloughs are on the rise; faculty are brought under tighter control as tenure-track positions are eliminated and two- or three-tier payment structures are implemented depending heavily on free or underpaid graduate students or temporary labor. These costs and hidden taxes only make sense if one considers education a product as opposed to a human right—if learning is a human right, it's a community responsibility; if it's metaphorically transformed into a product for sale, then market fundamentals apply. These tactics and strategies are consistent with an overall direction—the triumph of "academic capitalism"—that has characterized public higher education for decades: "restructuring" as biz-speak for a single-minded focus on the bottom line; the now common practice of selling public assets to profit-making enterprises; accommodating to relentless and escalating cutbacks in state support for colleges and universities; exploiting staff and student labor; carefully controlling access and tightly protecting class privilege; being complicit in gentrification; profiting from investments in war and prison and misery generally; disciplining and punishing an independent faculty; and entangling students with staggering debt. Higher education institutions are broke on purpose.

A few snapshots: state support for the University of Illinois system stands at about 16 percent, down from 48 percent two decades ago. In California state colleges will turn away 40,000 qualified students, while the community colleges, in a cascading effect, will turn away 100,000. A proposed 32 percent fee hike is on offer at the University of California at Berkeley (a proposal that triggered the student resistance), while the school pays its football coach $2.8 million a year and is just completing a $400 million renovation of the football stadium. The sportswriter Dave Zirin summed up this mess nicely: "This is what students see: boosters and alumni come first, while they've been instructed to cheer their teams, pay their loans, and mind their business."[2] A trillion dollars of student debt is a powerful disciplinary bludgeon—get in line, do your job, and shut up!

The meteoric rise of for-profit universities (and the eager university administrators trailing along while grasping their freshly minted MBAs) is another part of the trend; so are private universities competing to secure their advantages at the expense of their "competitors" at public schools as well as the public itself—Harvard, for example, with its ill-gotten $36 billion endowment. The brilliant public intellectual Erica Meiners pointed to Northwestern University (and its $7 billion endowment), whose new president had said that he was hoping to make his university "elite without being elitist," as she raised this pointed question: Exactly what "public" or "common" interest does this tax-exempt institution serve?

After World War II seven million veterans attended college or university and the country paid the tab through the

GI Bill—young people emerged debt free, and the benefit seemed broadly valuable. That benefit was reduced to a stipend in the decades that followed, but during the second Iraq invasion it was increased substantially (although never to its original breadth) and for-profit colleges were ready to strike, targeting veterans: they quickly sucked up millions of dollars in public funds while overstating job placement data, slanting attendance records, distorting grades, and creating classes that were inadequate and falsely advertised. For-profit colleges are far more expensive than community colleges, and students accrue staggering debt loads in order to attend. Ninety-six percent of students in for-profit colleges take out loans, and they owe an average of more than forty thousand dollars by the time they're done. Graduates from these predatory places have lower earnings than their community college peers, and they're much more likely to be unemployed. This is the market at work: The crimes and misdemeanors of the bosses at Corinthian and Anthem Colleges were so egregious that Congress investigated, and they were shut down. Student lawsuits are pending. Yet the for-profit colleges endure with government support.

But even this forbidding picture comes into more painful focus when we realize that California, for example, spends more on prisons than on higher education—across the country, spending on corrections is six times greater than spending on higher education—and from 1985 to 2000 Illinois increased spending on higher education by 30 percent while corrections shot up 100 percent. Here we get a clearer insight into the budget crises that are being rationalized and balanced on our heads: a permanent war economy married to a prison society, with education and health care kicked to the curb and the abused and neglected paying the ticket.

When the administration at UC Berkeley closed the libraries and restricted hours of operation to save money in 2010, students implemented a 24-hour "study-in" where they were joined by faculty as well as community members who had never before had access to a university library. Folks joined hands and chanted, "Whose university? Our university!" As one grad student said: "When we started we wanted to save the university; today we want to transform it, to decolonize it, to open it up."

Meiners argued that this moment of rolling crises is a time to seize, a moment to study up and act up, to speak out and reach out. It's a time for art and humor and creative interventions. And it's a time to envision the world we want to inhabit, and then to begin to live it, here and now, on campus and off. She suggested a few possible campaigns as starting points to get our creative and activist juices flowing: cancel all outstanding student debt (good enough for the banks, why not us?); equal pay for equal work (how about $25 an hour for all staff, including administrators?); truth in language (a furlough is not a camping trip, it's a pay cut; "selective admissions" is more honestly called *restrictive* admissions); universal free open-access high-quality public postsecondary schools (whew!). She also urged Illinois to create a single department to deal with spending public money to determine the life chances of citizens—call it UNISON, the merging of university and prison. It would be more honest.

✳ ✳ ✳

Canceling debt is a tradition that runs back through recorded time: a code of the Hebrews required that all slaves be liberated during their seventh year of service, and in the Bible (Leviticus 25:10) slaves and prisoners must be freed and debts forgiven in a Jubilee year—"a year of liberty"—for "it is a time of freedom and of celebration when everyone will receive back their original property, and slaves will return home to their families."

Fast-forward thousands of years to the dazzling anarchist thinker and activist David Graeber, a modern-day prophet perhaps, who has raised the banner of debt cancellation as a practical politics. He argues that humanity has an urgent need right now "to slow down the engines of productivity" because we are facing, he claims, two unsolvable problems that can only be viewed effectively and accurately as one colossal and frenzied crisis: On one hand, we have witnessed an endless series of global debt crises, which have grown only more severe since the seventies, to the point where the overall burden of debt—sovereign, municipal, corporate, personal—is obviously unsustainable. On the other, we have an ecological crisis, a galloping process of climate change that is threatening to throw the entire planet into drought, floods, chaos, starvation, and war. Debt is simply a promise—an agreement to pay off an advance at some future time. And the ridiculous and impossible contemporary situation is that humanity is promising itself that it will produce greater and greater quantities of goods and services than it does now, when it's perfectly clear that current productivity levels are completely unsustainable. We are destroying the planet at warp speed, and somehow we are promising ourselves, through debt, to accelerate the devastation. There's a simple solution at hand: cancel the debt.

Graeber believes that some form of Jubilee is inevitable, but the fight will be over what form it takes and who will feel the pain. He argues for cancellation of all global debt, a reduction of working hours to four hours a day with guaranteed five-month vacations. He can't be serious, you say, but he is. He thinks that kind of radical proposal could save the planet while allowing us to reimagine what value-creating labor might actually look like. Debt cancellation is a "perfect revolutionary demand" because it attacks the system at its ideological heart: "The morality of debt and the morality of work are the most powerful ideological weapons in the hands of those running the current system. That's why they cling to them even as they are effectively destroying everything else."

For the formerly enslaved workers and their families in the United States, that Jubilee year never came around, even after formal abolition. Poverty, disease, prison, unemployment, homelessness, and early death pursued people into the afterlife of slavery, and a legal and social system of debt peonage allowed the monied classes to ensnare workers in a web of financial obligations that foreclosed any hope of independence or liberty. Debt tracked folks everywhere (and it still does): A worker owed rent to live in a shack on the old plantation, bought basic commodities at inflated prices from the plantation store, leased tools from and sold his labor to the former owner—when the time for accounting came around, the worker was always deeper into debt. The predators ensnared African American households with shaky and dishonest loans in the 1980s and 1990s, and during the Great Recession 66 percent of inflation-adjusted Black wealth evaporated.

We want to live our lives now, to love our families and friends, to feel confident that we can secure for ourselves and our children the basics in life—food, shelter, health care, and education. And still we are always on edge: We aren't the big-time investors, yet our lives can be upended because of the inevitable booms and busts built into their financial system. We aren't the monetary wizards or the architects of the Ponzi schemes proliferating everywhere, but our hopes can be crushed when the bubbles they create periodically and inevitably burst. We aren't the big-time gamblers or casino owners, but speculation buzzes all around us and at the end of the day, on Wall Street just as in Las Vegas, when it's time to cash out, the house always wins and the predators will make off with their pounds of flesh. When the bubble bursts, the market collapses, and the economy crashes, the 1 percent land on their feet and walk away from the mess unscathed while many of the rest of us have lost our jobs, our homes, the value of our assets, our ability to pay our debts, and our confidence. The wreckage is all ours.

It's time to mobilize and build a Jubilee movement to cancel the debt! Blockade home evictions and suspend mortgage payments and all foreclosures pending a mass public forum on the banking practices that led to the housing crisis. Implement a moratorium on collecting debt payments from Third World nations in order to allow them to escape debt peonage. We need to come together and get smart about the rich and the rest of us. After all, we are many, they are few.

Five

Cops Index

Amount of military equipment transferred to local police forces, 1997–2014: more than $4.3 billion

Paid to citizens because of police violence or misbehavior in five years (2010–2014) in New York: $601 million
Chicago: $250 million
Los Angeles: $57 million
Philadelphia: $54 million
Baltimore: $12 million

Percentage of city budget dedicated to police in Baltimore (2011–2012): 20

Percentage of city budget dedicated to police in Oakland: 40

Number of civilian complaints concerning police misconduct in Chicago between March 2011 and September 2015: 28,567

Percentage of complaints that resulted in a police officer receiving discipline: less than 2

Laquan McDonald, a seventeen-year-old Black youth, was shot dead by a cop on the streets of Chicago on October 20, 2014. The official story follows a well-worn script: The police responded to a late-night call that someone was trying to break into cars and found a young man stabbing at the tires of a vehicle; when he refused to drop his knife and lunged at the officers, he was shot in the chest and died. He was one of nineteen Black men killed by Chicago policemen in 2014.

The names and the dates change, but the story does not—particular details and specific facts are stuffed neatly into a familiar and powerful narrative that organizes and circulates them: brave cops patrol a thin blue line between chaos and civilization, protecting the citizenry from explosions of random violence that pierce the calm. The bought media dutifully reports the police accounts of every incident without a nod toward independence or curiosity, typically with a stuttering tagline uttered that it was a clear-cut case of police acting in self-defense. The Independent Police Review Authority (IPRA), the agency charged with investigating police shootings, conducts an investigation, of course, as it does in every case of "police-involved shooting," and as always it concludes that the shooting is justified.

Pat Camden, longtime Chicago Police Department (CPD) press spokesman now with the police union, later described Laquan McDonald as "being a very serious threat to the officers, and he leaves them no choice at that point but to defend themselves."[1]

The scripted narrative is typically the end of it, but in this case it was cracked open and shattered by a social movement of young Black activists and by the tireless efforts of a couple of independent journalists. One of them, Jamie Kalven, founder of the Invisible Institute, a longtime police watchdog group, got an anonymous tip from a police source urging him to pursue the autopsy report. He later wrote: "An autopsy tells a story. The genre is mystery: a narrative set in motion by a corpse. The pathologist-narrator investigates the cause of death in precise, descriptive prose that ultimately allows the dead to testify about what happened to them. . . . It's very difficult to square the police narrative with the facts established by the silent testimony of Laquan McDonald's corpse."[2]

That silent testimony tells us this: Laquan McDonald was shot sixteen times in rapid succession, he died of "multiple gunshot wounds" from a single weapon, and several rounds entered his back as he lay on the pavement. (The other eighteen murdered by the police that year received ninety-three bullets collectively.) Everything smelled fishy. Tape from a surveillance camera on the roof of a nearby Burger King—seized by the cops—was found to have a gap at the precise time of the shooting. Jason Van Dyke, the cop who fired the shots, was assigned to desk duty and still on the payroll, while the city paid the McDonald family $5 million before a lawsuit was even filed. An anonymous tip led the journalists to pursue a dash-cam video from one of the several police cars on the scene. The city vigorously resisted, but in November 2015 a Cook County judge ordered the release of the video.

Suddenly, four hundred days after the murder of Laquan McDonald, the city sprang into purposeful action. The mayor held a press conference with the police chief where they denounced Van Dyke, fired him, and also recommended the firing of detective Dante Servin who in 2012 had shot and killed Rekia Boyd, an unarmed twenty-two-year-old Black woman. The state's attorney indicted Van Dyke for murder and explained that the timing was coincidental because investigations take time. Of course the city was in possession of the autopsy report and the video from the start, but the mayor was in a frenzy to reframe the story once the cover-up collapsed. And the video is the worst: A kid reeling down a wide, well-lit street late at night is corralled and cornered by several cops and cars; he looks toward the cops emerging from one car and veers away from them. He is executed.

That was not the end of it. This is the Black Lives Matter moment. Young people had been organizing and leading a grassroots movement opposed to police violence in Chicago for several years under various banners: Black Youth Project

100 (BYP 100), We Charge Genocide, Ella's Daughters, Project Nia, Assata's Daughters, the Chicago Freedom School. They had researched and documented police harassment and aggression, they'd gone to Geneva to present their findings before the UN Commission on Torture, they'd fought mass incarceration, they'd marched against school closings and joined the struggle for reparations for survivors of police torture, and they'd developed a comprehensive program of action that articulated a set of demands through a "Black queer feminist perspective," African American, womanist-powered, and gender/gay/lesbian/trans inclusive. BYP 100 cochair Charlene Carruthers said, "There's nothing unusual about the killing of a young Black person . . . by the Chicago Police Department. . . . We live in a city where the Chicago Police Department takes up 40 percent of our budget, while at the same time [they] close over 50 public schools. And so it says a lot to us about what and who our city prioritizes and who we don't." Community organizers, free spirits, artists and street activists, they would not let the issue or the memory of Laquan McDonald die. "We're calling for what we have always called for," Carruthers said. "We're calling for massive . . . defunding of the police and investment in Black communities. . . . We want full decriminalization of Black people in the city, be it for minor marijuana offenses or any other behaviors . . . our demands have not changed that focus squarely on defunding the police and investing in things like public schools . . . and we are committed to organizing to make that happen."[3]

In the past decade Chicago has paid out a stunning $500,000,000 in settlements for police abuse. The Invisible Institute recently won the release of tens of thousands of pages of civilian complaints filed against the Chicago Police Department—97 percent of which resulted in absolutely no disciplinary action. The Better Government Association reported that three hundred people were shot by Chicago police between 2010 and 2014—seventy people were killed. According to IPRA reports, Chicago police officers shoot, on average, one resident every week. Roughly 75 percent of those shot are Black, and, until Van Dyke, no cop had been criminally charged in almost half a century.[4]

The vindication of murder, execution, and serial assassination is part of a pattern of domination. In his classic short "teaching play," *The Exception and the Rule*, Bertolt Brecht tells the story of a rich merchant who journeys across the desert in order to complete an oil deal.[5] The merchant is accompanied on his trip by a porter (called the "coolie") and a guide. The merchant is increasingly brutal with the "coolie," and also frightened without the police nearby to protect him. The merchant and the "coolie" get lost in the desert and their water supplies run low, and when the "coolie" comes at night to share his remaining water, the merchant misinterprets his action, and shoots and kills the "coolie." In court evidence the judge concludes that the merchant had every right to fear the "coolie," and that he was justified in shooting in self-defense regardless of whether there was an actual threat or whether the merchant merely felt threatened. The merchant was acquitted.

The "coolie" is a victim of the rule of capitalism, like so many on the streets of America. The merchant is a proven murderer, but walks away free — like the assassins powered by an oppressive system. The exception and the rule.

Young Black people have dramatically reframed the serial killing of Black youth, naming, documenting, exposing, and challenging the rule of state violence. They have made visible the militarized police occupation of Black communities, and exposed the impunity with which police murder Black young (and not so young) people, and the institutionalized white supremacy embodied in the carceral police state. Black Lives Matter exploded into public consciousness as a radical social movement, but it did not fall fully formed from the sky.

In the wake of the assassination of Trayvon Martin in 2012, and his killer's 2013 acquittal, three savvy young Black women, Alicia Garza, Patrisse Cullors, and Opal Tometi, each experienced in labor, immigrant rights, and social justice organizing, had conceived of #BlackLivesMatter as a mobilizing tool, and this proved to be a critical flash of lightning in a gathering storm. Youth from coast to coast had been organizing for years around a range of racial justice issues, demanding work and living wages, immigrant rights, voting rights, adequate schools and educational opportunities, and an end to street harassment, stop-and-frisk, and mass incarceration. This emerging movement had been energized by grounded, community-based leader-organizers rather than charismatic or hierarchical leaders; it is not leaderless but "leader-full," in the words of Patrisse Cullors. The movement welcomed street theater, arts interventions, demonstrations, die-ins, and light brigades and, at its heart, required community organizing.

Black Lives Matter youth seek the widest participation and represent an open expression of the full range of community grievances and common dreams. Sparked by the additional police killings of Mike Brown in Ferguson, Missouri, and then Eric Garner on Staten Island—and the subsequent official findings in late 2014 that no one outside of the victims them-selves bore any responsibility for their deaths—the movement blew open a vast public space for organizing, education, ac-tivism, and dialogue. This violent assault on Black youth is nothing new—there is no documented national spike in po-lice violence. In fact, despite widespread criminal law data collection, there has been no US tracking of police shooting deaths. Black deaths at the hands of the state have been tacitly accepted as routine for decades by the capitalist media and too many white people, but now that eyes have been opened, we must choose sides, insisting Black lives matter and that Black youth never again be denied their childhoods.

Tamir Rice, a twelve-year-old out frolicking in a city park, was set upon and immediately shot dead by Cleveland police who described him as "menacing" and "in an adult body"; Rekia Boyd, an unarmed twenty-two-year-old Black woman, was shot in the head and killed by an off-duty Chicago police detective; Mike Brown, eighteen years old, was murdered by a policeman who described him as unstoppable, like "Hulk Hogan," and his body left to lie in the summer street for hours; Sandra Bland, a twenty-eight-year-old Black woman was stopped for "failing to signal when changing lanes" by Texas trooper Brian Encinia, who ordered Bland to put out her cigarette even though she was in her own car indulging her own legal habit, pulled her out of her car, and threatened her with a Taser: "I will light you up"—Bland was found dead in a Waller County jail cell three days later; Eric Garner was confronted for participating in the informal economy by selling "loosies," put into a choke hold and piled on by New York City police officers, and then recorded desperately pleading, "I can't breathe, I can't breathe," until he lost consciousness and died; the police murder of unarmed Samuel DuBose during a traffic stop was caught on camera in Cincinnati, Ohio. These cases and others like them have become the emblems of police occupation and official state terror and plunder. They reveal the links between racial injustice and economic exploitation and the correlation of a violent military system abroad to a colonial militarized police practice at home.

There are no excuses for ignorance about the killing of unarmed Black people, especially youth, at the hands of militarized, aggressive, and racially biased police forces. Say their names: Trayvon Martin, Amadou Diallo, Timothy Stansbury, Tamir Rice, Rekia Boyd, John Crawford, Alex Nieto, Aura Rosser, Eleanor Bumpurs, Oscar Grant, Walter Scott, Sean Bell, Fred Hampton, Victor Steen, Timothy Russell, Mark Clark, Orlando Barlow, Aaron Campbell . . . It does not end. We know that African Americans are twice as likely to be arrested and four times more likely to have force used while being arrested than whites; we know too that Black people are much more likely to die at the hands of police than are whites. We know that the criminal justice system is driven by federal policy and that court and jail systems from Ferguson to Chicago and from Baltimore to San Francisco are run on money squeezed from poor people through a system of civil as well as criminal harassment and peonage. We know that state violence is deployed selectively and systematically. We know all these things, and it's past time to wake up to reality and act out; silent recognition is simply complicity.

Police violence fits with the pervasive war culture on display everywhere and all the time. We find violent images and cultural artifacts at athletic events, where everyone is expected to sing ritualistic patriotic songs at the start and once again at half time or the seventh inning stretch, and where uniformed and armed people march with flags onto the field of play. The violent war culture is visible at airports and train stations where uniformed military people are given a designated waiting area and priority boarding. It's in our schools, where military recruiters have free rein. And it is in our language, where war metaphors hang heavy over all aspects of life, from sports and commerce to local politics and social policy, and where the word "service" has morphed quietly into a seemingly acceptable shorthand for time in the uniformed military.

War culture, combined with an ascendant and triumphant individualism, has led to legislation that contains a bizarre, catch-22 contradiction: "Stand your ground" laws allow anyone to shoot a person who seems threatening; "open-carry" laws allow people to carry guns openly—in a posture many would find threatening. What happens when a posse of open-carriers walks into a mall or a restaurant and meets a stand-your-ground crew?

Domestic debates about private gun ownership and gun control are dominated by Second Amendment mythmakers who insist that there's no common or collective possibility of public safety, and that it's each isolated person's individual right and responsibility to defend life and property and personal well-being with lethal force. The National Rifle Association (NRA) urges everyone to arm up, noting that the best defense against "a bad guy with a gun" is "a good guy with a gun." The NRA might consider introducing legislation (or passing devotional baskets in churches across the land) in order to offer a $1,000 stipend toward the purchase of guns to any American citizen or resident above the age of ten and living below the poverty line—there are many good guys among the young and the poor, and I've always gotten a kick out of the words scrawled across the Nightwatchman's guitar: "Arm the Homeless." Hell yes!

For those who prefer gun control, here's another alternative to arming everyone: disarm! To make the process fair and balanced, let's start with the hyper-violent US military, then move to our brutal domestic police forces, and finally the rest of us. Guns for everyone? Or guns for no one?

FBI director James Comey is usually quick on the draw when it comes to labeling acts of violence "terrorism" — after all, he has an annual $3.3 billion budget to counter terror — but he hesitated in the case of Dylann Roof's massacre of nine African Americans in the Charleston Emanuel AME church on June 17, 2015. Why? It was "horrific," he acknowledged, but "terrorism" is "more of a political act and . . . I don't see it as a political act."[6]

Really? The perpetrator himself saw it as a calculated and willful political act. His "manifesto" is a thoroughly articulated political document, one filled with apocalyptic fantasies and white supremacist daydreams as you're likely to find. And still Comey hesitates.

The farce of Comey's ambiguity is telling: It reveals the selective and hypocritical deployment of "terrorist/terrorism" as propaganda by the paid agents of the ruling class. Comey's FBI has labeled acts of vandalism "terrorism," including breaking windows, hammering on nuclear silos, disabling tractors in ancient forests or airplanes set to bomb civilians, freeing caged animals, and more. As a founding member of the Weather Underground in 1970, I know from close experience just how sweeping — and sticky — that label can become.

I'm reluctant to use the word at all — it flows so automatically into the rushing propaganda stream unleashed by the so-called war on terror, screaming insistently for a permanent state of war, more US aggression, more assassinations and torture, more ethnically based surveillance and repression, more suspicion and fear, more targeting of Arabs and Muslims. But I'll make an exception here: Dylann Roof is a white supremacist and a terrorist, his actions part of a long legacy of terrorism carried out against captured Africans and later their descendants. The history of organized terror against African Americans begins with the capture and kidnapping of Africans, tortured and transported to the Americas as chattel, none of them willing volunteers on the Middle Passage. This massive crime against humanity was state-sanctioned, legal terror.

Enslaved people ran away and resisted in a thousand ways, and after hundreds of years legal slavery was abolished. A decades-long campaign of terror against free Black people began immediately—pogroms, arson, displacement, false arrests and imprisonment, night riders, and thousands of public-spectacle lynchings. White gangs rampaged on a whim through African American communities in Chicago, St. Louis, Tulsa, Rosewood, and hundreds of other places, and the message was clear: White supremacy would police the racial boundaries and punish any transgression.

Dylann Roof's murderous outburst can be located in that long history of organized violence against African Americans to accomplish a political goal: the maintenance of white supremacy. The legacy continues, and the resistance is energized and mobilizing. Part of that resistance is to educate and organize around abolishing the whole structure of the war on terror, including the vague language that points toward indistinct enemies. There is no good reason to call for the state to pursue a terrorist enhancement charge against the terrorist Roof. He should and will be prosecuted to the full extent of the law. And we should continue to oppose endless war, the construction of a prison nation, mass incarceration, the militarization of the police, the serial murder of Black people, and state surveillance and repression.

The general narrative about police violence is that most cops are conscientious working-class men and women who are trying to help people, but a few "bad apples" mess things up sometimes. It's an attractive argument that lulls us into passivity and silence.

In reality the good guys are the exception, the well-intentioned volunteers whose presence disguises the core functions that have defined policing from the start. The first police forces, after all, were the Indian killers and slave patrollers.

In 2015 James Comey worried, he told audiences and media outlets across the country, that "a chill wind that has blown through American law enforcement over the last year," and it had led to an increase in violent crime. The police are being "sidelined by scrutiny," as the New York Times put it. "Lives are saved," Comey continued, "when those potential killers are confronted by a police officer, a strong police presence and actual, honest-to-goodness, up-close 'What are you doing on this corner at one o'clock in the morning' policing."[7]

You don't need to listen to the critics—Comey is up front with a clear statement about a particular police perspective on public safety and the place of the cops in a free society: Let the cops loose everywhere; let them do what they do without oversight or constraint or citizen/community scrutiny. Don't watch us. In fact, the culprit in Comey's perverse world has been Black Lives Matter. If "they" would just trust us, for chrissake, everything would be fine.

He brushed breezily past the ongoing murders of Black people by militarized cops and the state, claiming there were no reliable statistics. Actually there are: Read the *Guardian*—they have a counter running.[8] Comey condoned the fraternal camaraderie in every police department, a state of affairs that makes everyone there a participant in a vast conspiracy of silence.

This isn't new: The Black freedom movement was accused of creating civil unrest and disrespect for the law in the 1960s and '70s by reactionary politicians and racist police leaders. That was a lie too. But it's key to the agents of power to change the frame, to blame the victims of police murder, their allies, and the activists who rally in the name of justice and humanity. And it's key to our collective future to resist.

In our lifetimes, young people here and across the globe have risen up to challenge and change the world again and again: from Little Rock to Birmingham, Soweto to Tiananmen, Palestine to Chiapas, Wounded Knee to Tunisia. To be sure, youth were not alone in these struggles, but they were the ones who sparked the uprisings against vicious, repressive power. In the past decade, we've witnessed the Arab Spring, Occupy, and dazzling social movements for LGBTQ justice, immigrant rights, urgent climate justice, peace, labor rights, and reproductive rights. It's the youth who reject taken-for-granted injustices, and in this moment it's young people who are providing the insight and inspiration as catalysts, activists, and organizers.

With their radical impulse to revolt, a spirit of hopefulness and possibility, their laser-like insights into the hypocrisies of the adult world, youth are propelled to break the rules, resist collectively, and reimagine the world. They look at the status quo as unnatural and immoral—a state of emergency for the downtrodden, the marginalized, the exploited, and the oppressed. Inspired by the courage and determination of Ferguson youth, young people across the nation exercised their stubborn agency and walked out of schools, marched on police stations and city halls, sat in, died in, blocked highways and bridges—becoming the fresh, searing force for equality, racial justice, and dignity.

Black youth were not unaware of the risks they were taking by challenging police power and violence. In fact, young people were painfully and brutally aware of the police targeting of Black youth as well as the pervasive institutionalized devaluing of Black lives in the United States.

The moral activism of the Black Lives Matter movement—angry and loving—not only illustrates the brilliance and clarity of young people but also flies in the face of popular understanding that children and young adults are passive and disengaged, less competent, less thoughtful, less wise, and more dangerous than adults. The continuing reality of young people as social actors stands in opposition to official policies of silencing students, suppressing, searching, drug testing, expelling, and punishing our youth, depriving them of an education, and denying their creativity and their right to be heard.

Six

Health Care Index

Rank of United States among eleven wealthy
countries in health system performance (2013): 11

Rank of United States among the countries
of the world in annual per capita public and
private health care spending (2013): 3

Life expectancy in years of a typical US citizen (2012): 79

Rank of United States out of 224 countries
in average life expectancy (2015): 43

Administrative costs as a percent of hospital spending
in the United States/Canada (2011): 25.32/12.42

Number of Black/white deaths per 1000 in
the first month of life (2013): 7.46/3.34

Number of Black/white deaths per 1000 in
the first year of life (2013): 11.11/5.06

Number of Black/white children under two who contract
bacterial meningitis per 100,000 (2005): 26/11

Cost of Prevnar, a vaccine that prevents
diseases (ear infections, pneumonia) caused by
pneumococcal bacteria per dose (2014): $136

Amount of revenue that Pfizer, the monopolist and sole
manufacturer, realized from Prevnar in 2013: $4 billion

A perfect contradiction was on display in Washington, DC, in 2009 at a political rally called by the Tea Party Patriots. Participants came together in universal opposition to the Affordable Care Act, but their messages varied. "Obamacare Is Slavery," said one sign, and "Don't Tread on Me!" said another. There was also a large two-sided banner with one face reading "No to Socialist Medicine," and the other demanding that the government "Keep Your Hands Off My Medicare!" Of course, Medicare, like the Veterans Administration hospitals and the benefits that members of Congress enjoy, is predicated on something that most people want: good health and a health care system that delivers for all. Everyone is vulnerable to the vagaries and unpredictabilities of life, and so all of us benefit from the security that comes from being insulated from the financial shock of serious injury or illness, even if many of us will never suffer that fate; all of us gain when people get the low-cost health care they need at a price that we can jointly afford. It's not complicated. And it is indeed *mildly* socialistic—the system is still driven by profiteers and predators.

Those are the same ideas that motivate the drive for a single-payer health system: equalize the financial risk between the healthy and the sick, the well and the wounded, take all profit and market incentives out of the system, crush the health insurance racket, and create a simple social contract built on shared costs and guaranteed benefits. Medicare is an imperfect but sensible single-payer health care plan for the elderly and the disabled. It's similar in conception to national health care in Canada and throughout the industrialized world.

Of course Medicare—government-run health insurance for the elderly—was fiercely opposed by conservatives and political reactionaries when it was proposed half a century ago: "We are against forcing all citizens . . . into a compulsory government program," said one; it's nothing less than "socialized medicine," and, if implemented would mean that "one of these days, you and I are going to spend our sunset years telling our children, and our children's children, what it once was like in America when men were free."

That was the demigod of today's political right, Ronald Reagan, speaking before he'd entered electoral politics, and his comments echoed right-wing opposition to Social Security in the 1930s (a plan to "Sovietize America") and the minimum wage and mandated overtime pay ("Communism, Bolshevism, fascism and Nazism"). Here we go again.

Medicare has its problems, no doubt, many of them inflicted from the start by its opponents: It lacked a drug provision that could resist skyrocketing costs, and it prohibited preventive care like Pap smears and mammograms and flu shots for seniors (which it now pays), leading to more serious problems down the road, and making the emergency room—the worst place to receive primary care—the first stop for many people. Medicare pays for hearing exams for the elderly—50 percent of seniors have some hearing loss—but not hearing aids, so unless you have $1,500–$7,000 available, you go without. Twenty percent of people diagnosed with dementia, overwhelmingly poor people, are in fact suffering hearing loss.

Six times in the last several decades serious attempts have been made to develop and legislate a single-payer, universal health care system—Medicare for all! Each attempt failed, and each defeat relied on the powerful health predators and profiteers successfully coupling single-payer with "socialism," a political concept whose meaning has been so warped that it now connotes dictatorial, fascist, despotic, repressive, undemocratic, severe, tyrannical, top-heavy, bureaucratic, authoritarian, rigid, controlling, entangling, alien, foreign, French, orthodox, and godless governance by the Devil's own spawn. YIPES! WE'RE ALL GONNA DIE! No one wants that!

Yet people on Medicare express overall satisfaction with the system year after year, and compared to the tangled swamp of corporate medicine we slog through on our way to age sixty-five, it's no wonder. So, if Medicare is good for sixty-five-year-olds, why not sixty-year-olds? And if sixty, why not fifty? Down we go. It turns out that strong majorities favor just such a direction—some form of public option or single payer—but the corporate elites and their representatives in both major political parties wage a long and endless war on people's right to comprehensive health care. Some in the pay of the rackets push to privatize Medicare, others support increasing premiums and co-pays, chipping away at service, and shifting costs to working people. But none of them question the logic of the market or corporate medicine, and all of them allow the insurance and pharmaceutical industries to author or veto all health-related legislation. Big Pharma is in the business of business; health and wellness is the last thing on its agenda.

So the Tea Party banner demanding hands off my mildly socialist Medicare ironically rallies the troops against anything that smacks of affordable and available medical care for everyone. Other ironies abound: Americans pay two and a half times more per capita than other industrialized nations in health care costs, visit doctors less frequently than Europeans, go to hospitals less often, have fewer doctors per capita, experience lower life expectancy and childhood immunization rates, and are twice as likely to be deeply, deeply dissatisfied with their health care. The United States has more than enough money, state-of-the-art physical plants throughout the country, technology that is the envy of the world, twelve million health care workers, superbly educated doctors and nurses and technicians—and a shitty system. What went wrong?

The short answer: capitalism. Good medicine at its heart requires trust and an assumption of honesty and fairness; the market requires nothing more or less than profits for shareholders. The near-total corporate capitalist capture of health care incentivizes bad behavior: a primary care doctor ordering a battery of tests of questionable medical value because fee-for-service makes it profitable, or an obstetrician performing an unneeded Caesarian section because that procedure brings in more money only makes sense if dollars—and dollars alone—are the standard of care. Unnecessary medical tests (and procedures) are to the health industry what alcohol is to the hospitality industry: the Midas touch, everything turning magically to gold.

It's estimated that more than 90 percent of lower back pain cases are best treated with physical therapy, but doctors and hospitals routinely recommend expensive MRIs and then refer patients to orthopedic surgeons who often propose unnecessary, sometimes dangerous or harmful, and even more costly surgery. There's little profit in physical therapy, and, similarly, while home nursing is much more effective in treating chronic conditions like COPD (chronic obstructive pulmonary disease) and diabetes than hospital visits, there's no profit incentive in home nursing. And so it withers on the vine.

The health care marketeers lie in public, devise make-believe disorders and promote them through public relations and clever advertising, and then deal meds at the open-air drug bazaar to treat invented afflictions. Erectile dysfunction is now a fact of life, so I'll leave that one alone—except to note that Viagra is covered by Hobby Lobby's health care plan and birth control is not. But who knew millions of men are also suffering from a "medical condition known as low-T?" "Known as" by whom, you might ask; well, known as low-T by the drug runners who made the condition up. Here is their sales pitch: "If you're forty-something and just feel blah sometimes, out-of-focus, lacking energy, and not as charming as you thought you were at twenty, maybe it's not you . . . maybe it's low-T. Here, just apply this special under-arm deodorant filled with testosterone for a few weeks and you'll be the life of the party once more. Oh, and we should warn you to keep this out of the reach of women, children, and household pets, wash thoroughly after applying, and (*sotto voce*) be aware that this product may cause uncontrol-lable itching, hearing loss, temporary blindness, sneezing, hiccups, rectal bleeding, tumors, athlete's foot, dry mouth, suicidal thoughts, stroke, heart attack, hair loss, night sweats, crippling gas, adult-onset acne, attention deficit disorder, fe-ver, moodiness, frequent nose hemorrhages, gagging, facial tics, vertigo, burning sensations in your testicles—no worries, we have pills for each of those too. If you have an erection lasting more than seven days call this toll-free number and we'll rush you the antidote for that at reduced cost."

The United States is the only industrialized country in the world in which it's legal to advertise prescription drugs to the public. It serves no public health interest whatsoever, but it does indeed serve corporate wealth: antidepressants alone represent a $10 billion market; half of all Americans are tak-ing prescription drugs at any given moment, and one in ten is taking more than five; millions of youngsters are taking pre-scription drugs for ADHD, including fourteen thousand chil-dren ages two or three. We are all potential customers; even babies are the drug fiends the old dope peddlers hope to hook for the future. And the drug manufacturers have succeeded in laying the groundwork for an unprecedented heroin epidemic, which arose in part from the overprescription of opioids, or prescription pain medication, like OxyContin. It was reported in *Fortune* magazine in November 2011 that "254 million prescriptions for opioids were filled in the U.S."—enough to "medicate every American adult around the clock for a month," according to the federal Centers for Disease Control and Prevention (CDC). According to *Fortune*, opioids "generated $11 billion in revenues for pharmaceutical companies." This helps explain their fierce opposition to the relatively mild standards issued in early 2016 by the CDC in an attempt to address the record number of deaths from opioids in 2014: 28,647.[1]

The disorders are galloping forward, with the drug dealers conveniently on hand with just the thing to solve your problem. A headline in the satirical *Onion* warns of a growing epidemic among children that seems less and less farfetched: "An estimated 20 million U.S. children," it asserts, are believed to suffer from a "poorly understood neurological condition called YTD, or Youthful Tendency Disorder." The article details the early warning signs of YTD, including sudden episodes of shouting and singing, conversations with imaginary friends, poor impulse control with regard to sugared snacks, preferring playtime and flights of fancy to schoolwork, and confusing oneself with animals and objects like airplanes. A mother whose child was recently diagnosed with YTD expresses guarded relief: "At least we know we weren't bad parents," she says hopefully. "We simply had a child who was born with a medical disorder." She will be at the drug bazaar soon to get her kid hooked up.[2]

The market in health care has created a deeply unequal system that stretches from the shameful state of mental health care to the tawdry patchwork of nursing home care, from disdain for the poor to the war on women. The market—like all markets—creates winners and losers, and not surprisingly the biggest winners are the rich, and the biggest losers are those traditionally oppressed and exploited: descendants of enslaved people, First Nations peoples, recent immigrants from impoverished countries, people of color, women, and poor and working people. Health disparities are everywhere, and universally appalling: 25 percent of Black mothers get no prenatal care during the first trimester of pregnancy (and 6 percent get no care for the entire nine months) compared to 11 percent (and 2 percent) of white mothers; mortality rates during the first year of life are fourteen per one thousand for Black children and six per one thousand for whites; by the age of thirty-five months, 25 percent of Black children and 16 percent of white children have not received standard vaccinations; in poor Black urban neighborhoods in California there is one physician for every four thousand residents compared to one in twelve hundred in white neighborhoods.[3]

Martin Luther King Jr. noted, "Of all the forms of inequality, injustice in health is the most shocking and the most inhumane."[4] Health disparities focus a hard lens on our avowed values, revealing monstrous contradictions in a society that claims to value equality. It is wrong and shameful that one's zip code, for example, can be the strongest predictor of whether a person will suffer chronic lung disease.

Inequities between men and women are monstrous in the capitalist industrialized health system. Women's judgments about reproduction and birth are strictly policed by the state and the mobilized mob; this policing now includes a broadly accepted sense that a doctor and a hospital provide the best care during childbirth, while a mother is always cast as a potential risk to her baby or a danger to be managed ("Don't drink wine during pregnancy" and "Women of a certain age should always assume they are pregnant!"). Since 2011 more than 280 laws have been enacted in thirty-one states restricting women's access to reproductive health.[5] These laws make access more costly, more difficult (with mandatory wait times and multiple visits), and more humiliating.

Market-driven health care is also pauperizing us: 50 percent of personal bankruptcy filings in the United States are directly related to medical costs and bills. Industries from auto to airlines, as well as public entities from states to municipalities, claim they cannot meet financial or contractual obligations to employees because of the staggering costs of corporate health care. Compare Canadian and US auto industries and one thing stands out: health care as a contractual benefit (the United States) as opposed to a public trust (Canada) is extraordinarily stupid. US auto companies cannot meet the costs while a small segment of the organized working class is afforded a privilege that splits them off from other workers, and most people simply cannot track down adequate or reasonably priced insurance.

The market incentivizes corruption and fraud, and here's a case in point: Florida governor Rick Scott founded a holding company in 1987 and bought two El Paso, Texas, hospitals. Over the next several years he added hundreds of hospitals and medical centers, including Chicago's venerable Michael Reese, and in 1994 he purchased Tennessee-headquartered HCA and its one hundred hospitals and merged the companies to create Columbia/HCA. In 1997 federal agents announced that they were investigating whether Columbia/HCA had committed Medicare and Medicaid fraud. Scott immediately resigned as CEO, and three years later the Justice Department announced that the company he had founded and enriched himself with agreed to pay $840 million in criminal fines, civil damages, and penalties for among other things billing Medicare, Medicaid, and other federal programs for tests that were not necessary or had not been ordered by physicians, attaching false diagnosis codes to patient records to increase reimbursement to the hospitals, illegally claiming nonreimbursable marketing and advertising costs as community education, and billing the government for home health care visits for patients who did not qualify to receive them. The Justice Department settled a series of similar claims with Columbia/HCA in 2002 for an additional $881 million. The total for the two fines was $1.7 billion. Michael Reese Hospital was stripped and sacked—it went from 1,100 to 450 beds the moment Scott took it over, clinics were shuttered, and huge numbers of employees laid off until he took it into Chapter 11 bankruptcy protection, shaking off billions in debt, including $860,000 in unpaid taxes and $4.7 million in unpaid utility bills. Rick Scott was and still is very rich.

The market is also remarkably wasteful: An average nurse spends 33 percent of her time on documentation for insurers; the United States spends twice as much as Canada and Europe on administrative costs; 3 percent of Medicare costs go toward administration compared to 40 percent of individual insurance costs.

Our friend Joel Westheimer was visiting us from Canada when a phone book–sized document arrived for me in the mail explaining a set of choices and options I had related to my health insurance. He laughed and pulled out a plastic card from his wallet—his Canadian national insurance card. "This is it, and it's all I have," he said, a little meanly, I thought. "It includes dental, medical, drugs, vision, the whole kielbasa." As I worked my way through the book over the next few hours, Joel would occasionally look up from his laptop, smile patronizingly, and wave his card in my direction.

"Obamacare," the Affordable Care Act, delivered health care to millions—a good thing since life without health care is punishing in countless ways—but the cost was high: Health care was delivered even more firmly into the grasping hands of insurance and pharmaceutical companies, the idea that health care is a product (as opposed to a right) was more firmly entrenched, and affordable health care for all became an even more distant goal. Once the Obama administration abandoned some form of public option—fiercely opposed by the health profiteers—the game was up.

Walk-in clinics once ridiculed as "Doc in a Box" medicine have "mushroomed into an estimated $14.5 billion business, as investors try to profit from the shifting landscape in health care," according to the *New York Times*.[6] This is a hot topic on Wall Street as "private equity investment firms, sensing opportunity, invest billions in urgent care and related businesses." Patients are in and out in about thirty minutes and the average bill is $155 per patient per business. Do the math: "thirty or thirty-five exams a day and the money starts to add up." "Urgent care" has "a crucial business advantage over hospital emergency rooms," which are legally required to treat anyone who shows up: urgent care facilities refuse Medicaid patients and turn away the uninsured unless they pay cash upfront.[7]

The corporate health industry marches on: the price of childhood vaccines has skyrocketed in recent years. Pfizer, which has monopoly control over Prevnar, a vaccine that prevents diseases (ear infections, pneumonia) caused by pneumococcal bacteria, took in revenues of nearly $4 billion in 2013. Prevnar costs $136 per dose, and every child in the United States is required to have four doses before entering school.[8]

The market transforms a relationship of common interest into a relationship of antagonists. Pharmaceutical corporations lobby and win a provision in the drug law that prohibits the government from negotiating drug prices on behalf of the public, and bingo! Big Pharma reaps billions in profit. The market introduces deductibles, higher and higher co-pays, and restrictions and caps on coverage, and the market creates malpractice by developing an adversarial space between provider and patient. What was once human and natural becomes monetized and cheapened. Capitalism—the "free market," private enterprise—can't manage a decent health care system, and it never will.

Health care must be taken back from the grasping hands of the profiteers and taken to a higher ground appropriate to the project itself: everyone has the right to a standard of living adequate to health and well-being, including food and clothing, housing and medical care, and security in the event of circumstances (unemployment, sickness, disability, old age) beyond their control. Everyone has the right to lead a healthy life in a healthy community. Everyone has the right to life, liberty, and the pursuit of happiness—in the language of human rights, the highest available standard. It's time to organize ourselves to transform a system so blatantly destructive to these ends and institute a new community of associative living that will guarantee those rights to all.

On September 12, 2008, at a debate of Republican hopefuls cosponsored by the Tea Party and CNN, Representative Ron Paul was asked what our response ought to be to be if a thirty-year-old man who had chosen not to purchase health insurance found himself in need of intensive care. Mr. Paul said, "That's what freedom is all about—taking your own risks." Well, then should society let him die? A few in the audience shouted "Yes!" Just as Mr. Paul was quietly saying, "No," and elaborating that friends along with kindly medical folks and charitable groups might want to step in to help the lad.[9]

Political discussion and public policy often turn on questions of ideology expressed as competing comparisons that frame our points of view. If accepted common sense regarding health care holds that it's like any other individual consumer good—a television set or a radio—then our current system makes some sense. It taps into deeply held cultural beliefs about individual responsibility and cost, competition, and free enterprise. But if the analogy shifts, if health care is considered not so much a consumer product like all others but a universal human right, like the right to bodily integrity and public safety, then a different set of deeply held beliefs— about fairness and shared or community responsibility— move toward the front.

Challenging the insistent dogma of common sense is always a risky business—it involves disrupting unanticipated but linked fields, and it raises related questions: If universal health care is a human right, what else might be? If the accepted, market approach to doing health and medicine is suddenly suspect, what else in our public life is rendered unreliable? We enter an open space of rethinking and negotiation—a space where we must rely not on rules so much as on our moral intuition, our commitment to the dignity of persons, our belief in equality, and, yes, our reordered and evolving common sense.

Absent this capacity to raise risky questions and challenge the common conventions of our times, we would likely be burning witches and suffering slavery today. The capacity to wonder and to challenge belongs to all of us—making and remaking meaning is our acutely human condition—and it is the special province of rebels who are called to resist dogma, to expand inquiry, to raise queer questions. Our vocation is to try to shake free of the seductions and anesthetizing effects of the modern predicament, and that includes the seduction of common sense.

Let's flip the script and change the frame. Let's organize to replace cruelty and callousness with compassion, sister love, and fellow feeling. Let's fight to live up to the better angels of ourselves. Free and universal health care for all!

Seven

Education Complex Index

Annual per pupil budget allocation in District of Columbia Public Schools (2015–2016 academic year): $11,965

Annual tuition per student at Sidwell Friends School in Washington, DC (2015–2016): $37,750

Arts credits required to graduate from Sidwell Friends School (2014–2015): 2

Arts credits required to graduate from District of Columbia Public Schools (2014–2015): 0.5

Student-to-teacher ratio at Sidwell Friends School (2013–2014) 7.8:1

Student-to-teacher ratio in Washington, DC, schools (2013–2014): 13.32:1

Student-to-library-staff (professional and paraprofessional) ratio at Sidwell Friends School (2014–2015): 191.7:1

Student-to-library-staff (professional and paraprofessional) ratio in District of Columbia Public Schools (2013–2014): 710:1

In 1963 Charlie Cobb, a young field secretary with the Student Nonviolent Coordinating Committee (SNCC), wrote a brief proposal to create a number of Freedom Schools throughout Mississippi in order to revitalize the civil rights and community organizing work there. While the Black youth of the South, he argued, were denied many things— decent school facilities, honest and forward-looking curricula, fully qualified teachers—the fundamental injury was "a complete absence of academic freedom and students [that] are forced to live in an environment that is geared to squashing intellectual curiosity, and different thinking." He called the classrooms of Mississippi "intellectual wastelands," and he challenged himself and others "to fill an intellectual and creative vacuum in the lives of young Negro Mississippi, and to get them to articulate their own desires, demands and questions."[1] Their own desires, their own demands, and their own questions—for African Americans living in semi-feudal bondage and the afterlife of slavery, managed and contained through a system of law and custom as well as outright terror, this was a revolutionary proposal indeed, a giant leap of the radical imagination, and at the same time so completely characteristic of the Black freedom movement.

Andrew Goodman, James Chaney, and Mickey Schwerner were all SNCC volunteers engaged in the Freedom Schools. They had been investigating the arson bombing of a church that hosted one of the schools when they were arrested and jailed in June 1964; they were released into the dark of night, and then kidnapped and brutally lynched near Philadelphia, Mississippi, by the Ku Klux Klan, with the police acting as enablers and partners. The revolutionary meaning of the Freedom Schools wasn't lost on the rulers of Mississippi—their power and potential was understood well by the barbarians and their terrorist enforcers.

The world-shaking significance of the Freedom Schools —their prospects, legacy, and cost—should not be lost on us either. Let's begin by reiterating Charlie Cobb's premise for today: focusing on the young folks who've been written off and marginalized by the powerful and mainstream society. They are the descendants of formerly enslaved people or recent immigrants from poor countries or First Nations people. They're from working-class families—people who survive by selling their labor power, and even then frequently in the informal economy. They've attended schools of poverty, and many have participated in a sort of general strike and run away from those schools. They have endured institutions— not only schools but police and courts, hospitals, La Migra— that routinely refuse to recognize them, disregarding their humanity and denying their full personhood.

Now to restate Charlie Cobb's topic sentence: the youth of South Central LA or Detroit or Philadelphia or New Orleans or the West Side of Chicago are denied many things—decent school facilities, honest and forward-looking curricula, fully qualified teachers to work with them—but the fundamental injury is a complete absence of academic freedom. Students are "forced to live in an environment that is geared to squashing intellectual curiosity and different thinking." What would it mean and how would it look if they were to mobilize themselves in order to articulate their own desires, their own demands and dreams, and their own questions? I think the world would crack open—as it did in Mississippi—and in the best possible way.

This is because our radical imaginations are tenacious—they doggedly refuse to go quietly into that dark, dark night. When significant numbers of people are encouraged to pursue their curiosity and passion—when another world seems not only desirable to a large enough group but also possible—the status quo becomes suddenly unbearable, and revolution is in the air.

Black people in Mississippi knew that the Jim Crow system was unjust and cruel for a century; they'd suffered its lash and stood up where they could. They'd expressed their agency and resisted their oppression in a thousand clandestine ways—foot-dragging, absenteeism, sabotage—when they lacked the luxury of open politics. We admire the many overt refusals to go along—there were thousands of acts of open defiance to Jim Crow rules, on trains and on public buses, for example, that continually pushed the limits of what was possible and helped set the stage for that iconic action taken by Rosa Parks in 1956.

When a large enough group identified an obstacle to their humanity and chose to storm that impediment and overcome that barrier, when they collectively got the notion in their minds, for example, that if they risked registering to vote (a life-and-death proposition, an invitation to beatings and chain gangs) a more just world could be pried open for them and their children, and indeed for their entire community, the risk was taken, the battle engaged, and a wall was breached, releasing an irresistible tide—a revolution. There is no sound so sweet as the sound of chains that had held folks back for so long falling noisily to the ground. And it's still true: Once we can reimagine and resist in significant numbers, we will rise again, reaching for new heights and setting better foundations for living and loving, for building a new world.

The Mississippi Freedom School curriculum was organized around questions: Why are you and I in the freedom movement? What do we hope to accomplish? What would we like to change? The whole idea was to summon folks to name the circumstances of their own lives, to encourage them to a serious consideration of how those circumstances might be changed, and to invite them into space of authentic democracy and participatory action.

What do we hope to accomplish? What will help us realize our deepest dreams and desires? In what ways is education liberating, and it what ways can schooling be entangling and oppressive? Can learning be cast as a creative act, enjoyable and social, or is it always framed as competitive and brutal?

What does it mean to be an educated person? What does it mean to be free? Awakened to fundamental and forbidden questions, a new world of possibilities heaves into view.

In the Mississippi Freedom Schools, student experiences and student insights were a driving force in all the matters students and teachers inquired into and all the projects they undertook. Education was linked to life. No longer an abstraction, education became a vital matter of organizing and community empowerment. The main pedagogical gesture in Freedom Schools was dialogue—speaking with the possibility of being heard, and listening with the expectation of being transformed in some large or small measure. They offered experiences with dialogue, experiments in associative living, exercises in learning to live together, and a rich culture of recognition combined with a profound compassion for one another and our shared world.

I remember a class during which Stokely Carmichael wrote pairs of sentences on the board next to each other: "I digs wine" and "I enjoy cocktails"; "I be's unhappy" and "I am dissatisfied." He provoked a propulsive conversation about the power of language as a means of communication as well as a signifier of social position. The students walked away conscious of the codes of power and some of the invisible threads of oppression, and also with a stronger sense of their own capacity to name and change the world.

Students and teachers were set up to learn *from* the world, not about it; *from* fish and farming, construction and carpentry, gardening, history, and quantum mechanics—not simply about them. Freedom School classes studied voting patterns, property values, and health problems in the community. One class conducted a countywide survey of land ownership and made a chart tracing patterns of wealth transfer back to slavery. All of the classes were organized around learning by doing: interrogating, acting, producing, inquiring, and participating. No longer a set of anemic destinations, learning went deeper and traveled farther. And most important, students developed confidence in themselves as creators and meaning-makers in an infinite universe, not simply consumers of a static and unjust world.

The obsessions that characterize too many classrooms today—especially urban classrooms and schools attended by the poor—are simple: the goals are obedience, standardization, and conformity; the watchword is control. These schools are characterized by passivity and fatalism and infused with anti-intellectualism, dishonesty, and irrelevance. They turn on the familiar technologies of constraint—ID cards, uniform dress codes and regulations, surveillance cameras, armed guards, metal detectors, random searches—and the elaborate schemes for managing the fearsome, potentially unruly mob. The knotted system of rules, the exhaustive machinery of schedules, clocks, and surveillance, the unaesthetic physical spaces and the prison architecture, the laborious programs of regulating, indoctrinating, inspecting, disciplining, censuring, correcting, counting, appraising, assessing and judging, testing and grading—all of it makes these places feel like institutions of punishment rather than sites of enlightenment and liberation, places to recover from rather than experiences to carry forward.

The curriculum is flattened and lifeless in these spaces: in 2006 Florida passed the Florida Education Omnibus Bill, for example, stipulating that "American history shall be viewed as factual, not as constructed, shall be viewed as knowable, teachable, and testable." The bill called for an emphasis on the "teaching of facts." Facts and only facts—without any frivolous or messy interpretations—would be permitted to enter the schoolhouse. Facts and only facts would be allowed to guide instruction about, for example, the "period of discovery." Whose facts, exactly, I wondered? The facts of a Genoan adventurer in the pay of Spanish royalty, the facts of the "discovered" themselves with their complex stories of tribal rivalries, resistance, and accommodation, the facts of the First Nations residents overwhelmed, murdered, and enslaved, or possibly a range of other facts and angles of regard altogether? The Florida lawmakers went with the first choice, legislating in effect a pep rally for Christopher Columbus—yes, their own particular *constructed* explanation and analysis of events and circumstances passing as fact. It's deeply bizarre and mindlessly pinheaded, but it's a fact: In Florida the legislators banished debate and dialogue, independent inquiry and firsthand research, the right to think for oneself in a hurried scramble to paint a prettified picture of freedom and democracy in the name of fact.

✱ ✱ ✱

I watched a history teacher in a South Side Chicago school offer a standard lesson on the legendary 1954 Supreme Court case, *Brown v. Board of Education*, which reversed *Plessy v. Ferguson* and ended racial segregation in the United States. The classroom was made up of twenty-four African American students and seven Latino/a students. The lesson was pointedly directed toward illustrating our great upward path as a nation. A student who had appeared to me to be paying no attention at all spoke up rather suddenly, smiling broadly as he addressed the teacher: "So you're saying this class here is against the law? We're breaking the law here, right? Can I call the cops?" Everyone cracked up, but the disruptive student was pointing to an obvious contradiction: here was a segregated classroom in a segregated school in a country that had outlawed school segregation decades ago.

It doesn't take perceptive young people any time at all to sniff out the duplicity and the dirty-dealing approach in the nothing-but-the-facts agenda, and to conclude that all schools lie. Teachers lie. Parents lie. In fact the whole edifice of adult society is a complete phony, a tangled fraud sailing smoothly along on a sea of silence. Many students submit to the empire of deception, concluding that it's simply the price of the ticket: you wink at the massive hoax and promise to keep quiet and go along, and you'll pick up your reward by and by. Many other students go in the opposite direction: Their insights lead them to insurgent actions and gestures and styles, all matter-of-fact performances of self-affirmation, and hard-nosed refusals of complicity—flat-out rejections of a world that is determinedly disinterested in their aspirations and perceptions and insights.

As young people in New Orleans or South Central LA or Oakland or Philadelphia or Cleveland or many points in between discover and intensify their own sense of agency, they can start to see themselves as actors in the world and not merely adjuncts in society. Schools would be organized around an ardent faith in human agency—in individual as well as collective capacity. They would work to align themselves to children and youth in their infinite and dynamic diversity, as opposed to forcing the child to fit the school as if school were immutable and fixed in stone. Schools would embrace the truth that learning is the identical twin of living, that to be alive is to learn and to learn is to be alive.

No longer objects—instructed by people who tell them where they may or may not go, when they may or may not speak, what propositions they may or may not cross-examine, which books they may or may not read, when they may or may not use the bathroom, what time they may or may not eat, what materials they may or may not study—young people begin to question the nature of the schooling they're required to attend. In interrogating the real conditions of their lives they step out of subjugation and into history as subjects themselves. They realize as free and full human beings that they are inherently (and not contingently) valuable, that both they and the world they inherit are works in progress and still under construction, that as humans they are paradoxically completely unique and simultaneously the same as all others—we are all born into a human culture, we all experience pain, we all die—and finally that *they don't need anyone's permission to interrogate the world.*

They ask questions, all kinds of fundamental questions reaching out in every direction: why? Who decides? Who benefits and who suffers? Is it just? What are the alternatives? The act of questioning itself is understood by the wardens of the status quo as a challenge. The guardians are not wrong: To the oppressed and exploited, the status quo is itself an act of violence. It must be resisted, and questioning the circumstances of your life is a way to begin. To the wardens, the resistance must be quelled. The conflict is on.

The demands of youth will be heard above the roar: "I shall create," says the juvenile delinquent in Gwendolyn Brooks's masterful poem "Boy Breaking Glass," "If not a note, a hole / If not an overture, a desecration." The most fundamental human need/desire/demand is clear: I shall create!

The system dehumanizes everyone. Here is William Deresiewicz's description of the children of the privileged and the entitled: "These enviable youngsters appear to be the winners in the race we have made of childhood. But the reality is very different . . . Our system of elite education manufactures young people who are smart and talented and driven, yes, but also anxious, timid, and lost, with little intellectual curiosity and a stunted sense of purpose: trapped in a bubble of privilege, heading meekly in the same direction, great at what they're doing but with no idea why they're doing it."

A different fate awaits the less privileged: They are asked to submit to boredom and irrelevance like other students, and, further, some are required to endure racist behavior and daily humiliation, while others are rendered invisible by the institution and its managers as the price of the ticket. Their humanity is openly unacceptable, and they must prove their worth through abject compliance day in and day out. Privileged kids may see submission to a little monotony and irrelevance as a cost that will one day turn to an advantage for them—and they aren't wrong; other kids have ample evidence—an aunt, a neighbor, a cousin—that even should they submit and acquiesce and surrender, even if they reach for that highly touted diploma, there will be little or no payoff for them.

When the aim of education is the reproduction of all the social relations as they are now, schooling is nothing more than locating oneself on the grand pyramid of winners and losers. When school is geared to the absorption of facts, learning becomes exclusively and exhaustively selfish, and there is no obvious social motive for it. The measure of success is competitive—people are turned against one another, and every difference becomes a score for somebody and a deficit for someone else. Getting ahead of others is the primary goal in such places, and mutual assistance, which can be so entirely natural in other human affairs, is severely restricted or banned.

On the other hand, where questioning, studying, researching, and undertaking active work in the community is the order of the day, helping others is not a form of charity, an act that, intentionally or not, impoverishes both recipient and benefactor. Rather, a spirit of open communication, interchange, and analysis is an expression of love and becomes commonplace. In these places there is a certain natural disorder, some anarchy and chaos, as there is in any busy workshop. But there is also a sense of joy, and a deeper discipline at work, the discipline of getting things done and learning with one another and through life. We see clearly in these cases that education at its best is always generative—in a way that training, for example, never can be—and that offering knowledge and learning and education to others diminishes nothing for oneself.

In Freedom Schools students become conscious of themselves as authors of their own scripts, stars in their own dramas, sculptors of their own identities. They resist the objectification they suffered in society or in the miserable boot camps they knew as "school." They engage in naming the circumstances of their lives, holding hands and identifying obstacles to their full humanity and the humanity of others, and planning ways to collectively assault those obstacles.

In schools where teachers and students have their minds set on freedom, folks are encouraged and empowered to name and explain themselves, to describe their situations and their pathways, to bring their own wisdom and experience into the room, to wonder what's next and to act on whatever the known demands. Human agency finds its rightful place at the center of the educational experience.

* * *

Education is a fundamental and universal human right: something every child deserves simply by being born, a moral obligation of the community, a phenomenon resting on the twin pillars of enlightenment and liberation, and principally directed to the fullest development of the human personality. That's a starting point.

Education for free people is powered by a particularly precious and fragile ideal: *Every human being is of infinite and incalculable value,* each a work in progress and a force in motion, each a unique intellectual, emotional, physical, spiritual, moral, and creative force, each of us born equal in dignity and rights, each endowed with reason and conscience and agency, each deserving a dedicated place in a community of solidarity as well as a vital sense of brotherhood and sisterhood, recognition and respect. Embracing that basic ethic and spirit, people recognize that the fullest development of each individual—given the tremendous range of ability and the delicious stew of race, ethnicity, points of origin, and background—is the necessary condition for the full development of the entire community, and, conversely, that the fullest development of all is essential for the full development of each

This has obvious implications for educational policy: racial segregation is wrong, class separation unjust, disparate funding immoral, relentless privatization an assault on the commons and the community. There is simply no justification in a democracy for schools dependent on local property taxes, or for the existence of one school for wealthy white kids funded to the tune of $50,000 per student per year and another school with access to less than $5,000 per student per year. That reality offends the very idea that each person is equal in value and regard, and reflects instead the reactionary idea that some of us are more deserving and more valuable than others. It also expresses a simple but crude and cruel message to young people: Choose the right parents! If you choose parents with money, access, social connection, currency, and privilege, your chances will expand; if not, sorry, but social policy favors the comfortable—you're on your own.

A common faith in the incalculable value of each human being has big implications for curriculum and teaching as well, for what is taught and how: Freedom lovers want students to be able to think for themselves, to make judgments based on evidence and argument, to develop minds of their own, and most of all, to become free people themselves, capable of participating fully in the world as it is, and, if they choose, transforming all that they find before them in order to create a new and better world.

Schools for obedience and conformity are characterized by passivity and fatalism and infused with anti-intellectualism and irrelevance. They turn on the little technologies for control and normalization—the elaborate schemes for managing the mob, the knotted system of rules and discipline, the exhaustive machinery of schedules and clocks and surveillance, the laborious programs of sorting the crowd into winners and losers through testing and punishing, grading, assessing, and judging, all of it adding up to a familiar cave, an intricately constructed hierarchy—everyone in a designated place and a place for everyone. In these schools, knowing and accepting one's pigeonhole on the towering and barren cliff becomes the only lesson one really needs.

Free people, including free teachers and free students, refuse obedience and conformity in favor of liberating dispositions of mind: initiative, questioning, courage, audacity, imagination, creativity, inventiveness, and empathy. These qualities cannot be delivered in top-down ways, but must be modeled and nourished, encouraged and defended, and mostly practiced again and again and again.

Free students are major actors in constructing their own educations, not simply objects of a regime of discipline and punish; they demand that education become decoupled from the inadequate and illegitimate "meritocracy model," and that the public good become understood more fundamentally. Instead of schooling-as-credentialing, sorting, gate-keeping, and controlling, education for freedom enables *all* students to become smarter and more aware, more capable of negotiating our shared and complex world, more able to work effectively in community and across communities. This requires courage —from teachers, families, communities, and students—to build alternative and insurgent classrooms and schools and community spaces focused on that we know we need rather than what we are told we must endure.

Educators who are oriented toward liberation and enlightenment as living forces and powerful aspirations focus their efforts, then, not on the production of things but on the production of fully developed human beings who are capable of controlling and transforming their own lives; citizens and residents who see themselves as valued and valuable, a sovereign part of the whole, participating actively in public life; people who can open their eyes and awaken themselves and others as they think and act ethically in a complex and ever-changing world. This kind of teaching encourages students to develop the capacity to constantly interrogate the world and the courage to act upon whatever the known demands. Education, then, is transformed from rote boredom and endlessly alienating routines into something that is eye-popping and mind-blowing—always opening doors and opening minds and opening hearts as students forge their own pathways into a wider world.

When education is posited as a product like a car or a refrigerator, a box of bolts or a screwdriver—something bought and sold in the marketplace like any other commodity—and schools are conceived as businesses run by CEOs with teachers taking the role of assembly-line workers and students playing the part of the raw materials bumping helplessly along the factory floor as information is incrementally stuffed into their little upturned heads, then it's rather easy to suppose that "downsizing" the least productive units, "outsourcing" and privatizing a space that once belonged to the public is a natural event. It seems logical in that universe to transform proof of learning into a simple standardized metric where state-administered (but privately developed and quite profitable) tests determine the "outcomes" and act as a rational proxy for learning; where centrally controlled "standards" for curricula and teaching are made commonsensical; where "zero tolerance" for student misbehavior is a stand-in for child development or justice; and where "accountability," that is, a range of sanctions on students, teachers, and schools—but never on lawmakers, foundations, or corporations—is transformed into something logical and level-headed. This is in fact what a range of corporate bosses, their noisy politicians, and chattering pundits in the bought media call "school reform."

The forces fighting to create this new commonsense; school reform normal are led by a merry band of billionaires—Bill Gates, Michael Bloomberg, Sam Walton, Eli Broad—who work relentlessly to take up all the available space, preaching, persuading, and promoting, always spreading around liberal amounts of cash to underline their fundamental points: dismantle public schools, crush the teachers' unions, test and punish.

What if this school/classroom/experience were for me, or for my child? Are these the schools a free people require? This is a clarifying starting point for discussion: If it's not okay to cut the arts or sports programs, the clubs or libraries or science labs for your child—or for the children of privilege—how can it be okay for the children of the poor? If you want teachers for your kids who are thoughtful, caring, compassionate professionals—well rested and well paid, completely capable of making clear and smart judgments in complex situations—how can you advocate for teachers who are little more than mindless clerks for the children on the other side of town? If your school doesn't face the constant threat of budget cuts and schedule changes, why should other schools and educators live in that tumultuous and disruptive environment? We should be highly skeptical of reformers—whether Gates or Bloomberg or Bush or Obama—who claim to know what's best for other people's children when it would be unacceptable for them or for their precious ones. This kind of test can be easily applied.

Teachers, like their students, are in transition, in motion, works in progress. In the Freedom School tradition, teachers become students of our students, in part to understand them, in part to know ourselves. A powerful reason to teach has always been to learn ourselves, and no one captures this more beautifully than Paulo Freire: "Through dialogue the teacher-of-the-students and the students-of-the-teacher cease to exist and a new term emerges: teacher-student and students-teachers. The teacher is no longer merely the-one-who-teaches, but one who is himself taught in dialogue with the students, who in turn while being taught also teach. They become jointly responsible for a process in which all grow."[2]

This challenges the manufactured image of good teachers as child-savers and lone heroes heavily promoted by the corporate gang and reflected in films and newspapers. My favorite parody of this whole mess is a short piece from MADtv available on YouTube called "Nice White Lady." It opens as a camera hovers over an urban landscape and the narrator intones: "Inner-city high schools are a dangerous place . . ." The camera enters a classroom where kids of color are lounging at their desks cleaning their firearms and sharpening their knives. The narrator again: "Only one thing can help these kids learn . . . a nice white lady." A young, fresh-faced woman appears and announces, "My name is Amy Little; I'm a white lady." The kids sneer and jeer, and later, one young woman is right up in the teacher's face with maximum urban attitude. She growls as she rattles off why her life is difficult and how she won't be inspired by the white lady teacher. Amy is at first taken aback, but then a light bulb goes off, and she hands the student a notebook with the command: "Write that down!" Soon everyone is writing and winning literary awards, trading their guns for pencils, and the narrator concludes, "When it comes to teaching inner-city minorities, you don't need books and you don't need rules. . . . All you need is a nice white lady."[3]

Recognizing the full humanity of every person is an essential part of resisting corporate school reform. The teacher notes that every human being has a unique and complex set of circumstances that makes his or her life understandable and sensible, bearable or unbearable. Each student is the one and only, and, paradoxically, each is the one of many. This recognition asks teachers and schools to reject any action that treats anyone as an object, any gesture that thing-ifies human beings. It demands that we embrace the humanity of all students and that we take their side.

To imagine schools as they could be or should be, schools that embody and express love, joy, and justice, is to dream of a world fit for all. It's to resist the dystopian metaphor of education as a market in favor of education as a basic right.

It's to unite parents and children, teachers and community members in a gigantic organizing and mobilizing effort to rebuild and expand the commons and the public spaces of education; to abolish privately developed high-stakes standardized tests in public schools, and to cease and desist from valorizing test scores as a proxy for either intelligence, worth, or achievement as we move toward authentic forms of assessment; to ban privately managed schools from receiving any public funds; to end the criminalization of youth and open alternative spaces for creative moral reflection and positive action, redemption, and recovery, whenever and wherever someone has made a mistake or wronged the community; to pay every public school teacher a salary comparable to the average pay of a US general; and to enact a massive initiative to bring parents, community characters, formerly incarcerated people, and unemployed folks into the schools as aides and teacher candidates, and to bring students, teachers, and other school people into communities as peers and colleagues, oral historians and arts innovators, coaches and team-builders. We come together, then, to release our radical imaginations in the service of a future world of enlightenment and freedom for all.

In 1967 at the age of fifty, with the rat-tat-tat of revolution in the air and an exuberant sense of change sweeping throughout the whole world, Gwendolyn Brooks—with several books of poetry, a novel, and a Pulitzer Prize under her belt—wrote of the grand rebirth of consciousness during the early days of the Black Arts Movement: "I who have 'gone the gamut' from an almost angry rejection of my dark skin . . . to a surprised queenhood in the new black sun—am qualified to enter at least the kindergarten of new consciousness now. New consciousness and trudge-toward-progress. I have hopes for myself."[4]

"New consciousness and trudge-toward-progress"—we're reminded that it is only the urgency of youth that can set the pace and the tone of what is to come—of what is to be done— and still, in the grace and fullness of age we might learn to follow along, to enter at least the kindergarten of the new. Because I have hopes for my students and my young friends. Because I have ambitions for my children and my grandchildren, I also have hopes for myself.

Eight

Earth Index

Monsanto Company's annual budget lobbying the US government (2015): $4.3 million

Year the FDA approved Monsanto's bovine growth hormone (rBGH)—banned in thirty-one countries—for use in American cattle: 1993

Profits made in the decade from 2001 to 2010 by the top five oil companies: $901.6 billion

Profits ExxonMobil averaged each quarter in 2012: $11.225 billion

Percent of combined $100 billion 2008 profits the big five devoted to "renewable and alternative energy ventures": 4

Percent rise in water utility rates for average Detroit resident in 2015–2016: 9.3

Estimated number of Detroit residents affected by water disconnections (as of July 2014): 100,000

Value of the Detroit Water and Sewerage Department (DWSD): $6.4 billion

Percent of the DWSD budget that goes to Wall Street banks as debt service (FY 2016): 45

Amount contracted to Homrich, a private contractor hired to disconnect water from Detroiters whose overdue bills exceed $150: up to $5.6 million

Two young steelheads are happily swimming downstream when they pass an old crab sitting on a rock in the cool mud beside the river. "How's the water?" asks the crab. The young fish look at one another blankly. "What's water?" they ask.

That's an old and universal story, and its meaning is evident: the fish are the last to notice or to be able to describe the water, whose dimensions — texture and temperature, chemical code, resonance and resistance — nonetheless constitute their whole world. Because they live within the water, it's entirely taken for granted; because they can't quite imagine a nonwatery world, they have a limited and distorted view of their own home.

The taken for granted, as always, exercises a powerful pull: It's difficult for some city-dwellers in the West, for example, to comprehend drought — even severe drought — as long as water pours from the tap (as it always has in their experience) whenever the faucet is opened. They will have to step outside their increasingly nonwatery world if they will ever develop a truer and more accurate picture of their own closing habitat.

Our own human steelheads today, however, are driven by more than innocence or naiveté—evidence of cataclysmic climate change and environmental collapse are all around us, easy to see and to understand wherever you look: the raging fires and the freakish storms, the droughts and the floods, the climbing rates of extinction, the stressed-out birds or the fading bees, the frazzled fish or the misshapen frogs, the temperature, the air, the water. It takes some bizarre combination of self-interest, privilege, cynicism, ideology, corruption, dogma, or chutzpah to keep one's head buried in the sand, denying the facts in favor of cloud-cuckoo-land fantasies. But denial is not just a river in Egypt, no—magical thinking is the name of the game for the cataclysmic climate change deniers, our own steelheads.

This magical thinking takes many forms. Climate change is a theory—that's the first line of defense for the steelheads—and the science is disputed. Climate is always changing, and has for millennia—second line of defense—and anyway, it's in God's capable if mysterious hands. Egads! Okay, it's getting warmer, but the causes are complex and unknowable—third line, moving backward—and you can't prove that it's caused by human beings. In any case, ingenuity, the free market, and technological advances will work out the kinks as we become ever bigger and better and more prosperous forever. Finally, misdirection and an appeal to anti-intellectualism: Don't trust the "liberals" and their pesky friends, the "scientists."

All of this is nonsense and demonstrably bogus. Since the industrial revolution began, the Earth has warmed 0.85

degrees Celsius, and 2013 was the thirty-seventh consecutive year of above-average global temperatures. In May 2014, the hottest May ever recorded worldwide, the average temperature was 0.74 degrees Celsius above the twentieth-century baseline. And 2015 was the hottest year since temperatures have been recorded. At this rate we will experience a six-degree Celsius increase by 2100. Anthropogenic climate disruption (ACD)—human-produced climate change—is a fact of life. But facts haven't a chance in the face of orthodoxy, and the steelheads peddle a toxic brand, fact free and faith based.

The three-term governor of Texas, a state on fire, has campaigned repeatedly and noisily against any environmental restrictions that would impact Big Oil or Big Energy. He's a poster boy for steelheads. So is Senator Ted Cruz, who organized prayer circles during a crippling drought. You can imagine the governor looking distantly out the window of his mansion with those vacant steely eyes and observing that the earth is plainly flat as far as he can see, or, as he might put it, "Hey, why am I not upside-down?" Oh, you are governor, you are.

But there's much more. "I'm no scientist," he concedes as he pockets another payment from the filthy extractors and the profit-hungry polluters. He vehemently opposes regulations that would cut carbon emissions or policies that would constrain expanding oil and gas exploration because these are essential to "economic opportunity" and "energy independence" adding that "CO_2 is not a pollutant!" This gets closer to the deeper point and the most critical line of defense: The scientific truth of climate change is a side issue for the most

dedicated steelheads, including the senator and the governor; it's the actual implications of what has to be done to halt
the unfolding catastrophe that sends them rallying fervently
around the flag, each of the fifty state stars now morphed into
a colorful corporate logo.

What is to be done? Struggling with that question illuminates
the strongest argument the steelheads have, even as it exposes
their point of greatest vulnerability: seriously engaging the
environmental catastrophe, and taking the necessary steps to
solve it, will mean — I'll just spit it out here — overthrowing
capitalism. This is the real choice in front of us: the end of
capitalism or the end of the habitable Earth, saving the system
of corporate finance capital or saving the system that gives us
life. Which will it be?

One of the "secret joys," as Rebecca Solnit puts it, of
fighting to save Earth hand in hand with indigenous peoples
around the world and the massively expanding environmental movement, is knowing that doing the right thing eco-
logically has huge rewards socially as well.[1] Spreading the
practice of decentralized power generation through rooftop
solar, for example, points away from corporate-driven policies and toward participatory and power-dispersed solutions
in every area: food production, transportation, health matters,
and more. In other words, if we collectively enact grassroots,
participatory, and transparent solutions to the crisis in a single
area, we expand our consciousness, our radical dreams and

aspirations, and our community capacity in other areas. We open to a wider world of participatory democracy.

The steelheads can deny the reality of catastrophic climate change all they like, but the hardheaded realists in the corporate board rooms, the Pentagon, and the State Department have done the studies and drawn the maps. They have strategies and tactics already laid out: permanent war, more mobile rapid attack forces, higher and higher walls around fortress USA, technological solutions to decidedly nontechnical problems, an amped-up nationalistic patriotism with its attendant chauvinism and white supremacy, a frenzied appeal to individualism, and the demonization of anyone who rises in opposition.

The usually reliable but increasingly fragile playbook to save capitalism includes massive propaganda campaigns designed to dupe and deceive, to narrow and frame the debate so that it appears that *there is no alternative* to the logic and practice of avarice and predation. Violence and aggression will be framed as inevitable—invasions and conquest, long-term occupations to secure diminishing resources, wars for oil and raw materials and, coming soon, water wars—and any resistance here or abroad will be cast as the wicked work of terrorists or fanatics. The victims of the catastrophe created by late capitalism—there are millions of climate refugees already on the move—will be labeled "illegal aliens" or "lawbreakers" and put in concentration camps beneficently renamed "temporary holding centers for the undocumented."

Capitalism demands expansion; its predatory heart is the rage to accumulate. It thrives on growth unleashed and unrestrained, but Earth says otherwise. It reminds us of our shared responsibility and stewardship, of our public obligation to supervise and check and intrude when the private pursuit of profit threatens us all. It's admonishing us: The ecological burden of unchecked economic growth is simply too much; learn to proceed with caution and constraint—slow down or die. No one can predict with any certainty what is to come; no one can name the mode of life or the institutions we will build in order to assure survival; no one can plot out a clear path forward. But the window is closing, and an entirely new condition is upon us. We will awaken soon enough to the society that must emerge if we are to survive, or we will witness complete collapse. There may still be time left: we can lie down in defeat, or we might rally ourselves to storm the heavens.

The steelheads are counting on people being too short-sighted or self-interested or mystified or mesmerized or frightened or intimidated to choose life. The people—this is the X factor and the wild card, their Achilles's heel and our potential lifesaver—with our marvelous unpredictability and our unscripted potential, our infinite capacity to step into history at any moment as subjects with hearts and minds of our own. The steelheads' greatest fear is our best hope—collective consciousness, common struggle.

In *The Shock Doctrine*, the dazzling thinker and writer Naomi Klein produced a germinal account of how corporate power, the 1 percent and their flacks in the media and political establishment, systematically use crises, both real (like floods or fires) and invented (like Detroit going bankrupt), to enact cruel ideological agendas designed to enrich themselves at the expense of those who were hurt by the problems in the first place. Disaster capitalism seizes every tragedy, misfortune, or calamity and turns it into just another profit-making opportunity. The real causes of crises are never examined by the powerful, authentic or alternative solutions never seriously pursued, as the elites double down on the very policies and politics that created the messes in the first place.

Klein's latest book, *This Changes Everything*, with an accompanying documentary film by her partner and comrade Avi Lewis, is an urgent cry to wake up—get woke!—and pay attention to the dangers facing us and the pressing need for thoughtful and genuine alternatives. Together they rally us to put the scientific reality of catastrophic climate change into all of our movement-making efforts, and to build a coherent and unifying narrative about the real solutions to the climate crisis—an enlightened economic system capable of restraining corporate power and capitalist avarice, strengthening participatory democracy, sharing Earth's limited resources, and discovering ways to unleash our energies to do the real and necessary work of the world uncoupled from the jobs system and racism and wage slavery.

Klein and Lewis insist that climate change is not an issue like every other; in fact, it's not an issue at all. *Climate change is a message*—and that message literally changes everything. Climate change is instructing us on the limits and

the interconnectedness of nature. It is challenging our arro-
gance; it is revealing that the inherent and intrinsic value of
nature cannot be monetized or marketed without irreparable
harm; it's telling us to reimagine how we live, what we value,
how we see and treat one another, and how we organize our
labor; it is asking us to invent and discover sustainable alternatives; it's urging us to pay attention, be astonished, and act!

Painting capitalism green won't help. The capitalists
merely invent markets to trade carbon and other pollutants,
or keep our eyes fixed on individual behavior rather than systems, as the crisis continues gathering steam. State capitalism
or command-and-control socialism won't help either—those
systems run hungrily and recklessly on retrograde notions of
progress, carelessly damming rivers, hastily extracting all the
coal and gas they can grab, heedlessly burning filthy fuels,
expanding, growing, accumulating whatever they can as far
as they can reach.

With cataclysmic climate change in focus, Klein and
Lewis offer a more hopeful agenda: we must all work to reimagine and vitalize the public square, spaces where people
can face one another without masks and participate fully in
planning the urgent work of creating human-sized solutions
to the crisis. We must turn back the frenzied drive to privatize; we must regulate and tax banks and corporations heavily,
and get popular public control where we can; we must resist
overconsumption and rely more heavily on local production;
we must disarm and drastically reduce the size and scope of
the military as we face our debt and our responsibility for the
problems of poor and developing nations. We might look to

the recent gatherings on climate change in Paris, Cochabamba, and Cancún, where many of these ideas were center stage, and welcome the seizing of global environmental leadership by the marginalized and the many from the powerful elites.

This is a broad agenda to be sure, but it's also entirely within reach. We see stirrings in patches everywhere: Occupy, of course, with its brilliant metaphorical victory—We Are the 99 Percent!— and its broad and inclusive appeal; the activists of Black Lives Matter connecting criminal justice reform with educational and environmental justice; "take back the land" actions, from Miami to Chicago; squatters in Seattle and Boston; alternative systems for health and medicine, food production and distribution, transportation, public safety and housing in Detroit and Oakland and Milwaukee and Chicago; protests, encampments, resistance, strikes, blockades, sit-ins and walkouts and occupations everywhere. These are the seeds of a new world: instead of me-first-ism, recognition of interdependence and a faith in community; instead of monologue, dialogue; instead of worshipping power, an ethic of care and generosity and compassion; instead of easy answers, hard questions; and instead of domination, cooperation and reciprocity. It's not a big stretch to imagine a seemingly isolated protest in a sweatshop in China, or a blockade by miners of a copper pit in Chile, or a farmworker land seizure on a plantation in Guatemala, or an encampment in the Central Valley of California triggering a worldwide upheaval to reclaim Earth. If you open your senses a bit, you can feel the rumblings coming closer.

Klein and Lewis are clear that while "there is no joy in being right about something so terrifying," it does point to a deeper duty for all of us. The responsibility now is to become clearer and more focused about challenging the profit-driven system at its root as the "best hope of overcoming these overlapping crises."

In Don DeLillo's grimly funny and super-smart novel *White Noise*, the narrator is Jack Gladney, a professor of "Hitler Studies" at a small Midwestern college. Jack sleepwalks through his life to the dull background sounds of TV and endless radio, the Muzak of consumerism and electronics, unrestrained advertising and constant technological innovation, appliances and microwaves. Jack is a steelhead with intellectual baggage. When a train derails outside of town creating what is at first described officially as a "feathery plume" but later becomes a "black billowing cloud" and finally an "airborne toxic event," everything becomes a bit unhinged. Jack's response to an official evacuation order is disbelief: "I'm not just a college professor," he complains. "I'm the head of a department. I don't see myself fleeing an airborne toxic event. That's for people who live in mobile homes out in the scrubby parts of the county, where the fish hatcheries are."

Well, not anymore. Our own feathery cloud has turned toxic at breathtaking speed, and those folks in the mobile homes might be our best natural allies after all.

We are each other's harvest
we are each other's business
we are each other's magnitude and bond.
                                —Gwendolyn Brooks

former US secretary of state Madeleine Albright famously asserted that the United States is the one and only "indispensable nation." "If we have to use force, it is because we are America," she said. "We are the indispensable nation."[1]

A benign interpretation of that extravagant claim might visualize the country as the protector of freedom, a shining city on the hill and a paragon of democratic values and human rights. A more execrable interpretation might see the United States astride the world like Colossus, holding itself exempt from international agreements (for example, on the environment, the international criminal court, women's liberation, children's rights, the elimination of racism and xenophobia, human rights, and nuclear disarmament), above the rules that govern all others, particularly concerning the use of lethal force against other nations or peoples. In her own mind Albright may have conflated the two: because we are the good guys, models of virtue and righteousness, our actions will always be good; because our actions are always good, we are not subject to ordinary restrictions that apply to every other nation and people, such as international law; because we are above the law, rules and statutes and sanctions are applied selectively, in our favor, and against the bad guys. Back to the start: We are the good guys. In other words, if the United States takes an action, it is by definition good. We are the indispensable nation—the naked narcissism is widely shared and entirely Trump-worthy.

All patriotism in all places includes the manufactured or imposed capacity to see similar sets of facts in dramatically different ways. Torture, rendition, imprisonment without trial, economic plunder of natural resources, seizure of strategic waterways, domination of the air and the seas, invasions and occupations, extrajudicial killings, assassinations, drone strikes, and the bombing of civilians—all of these atrocities and more are condemned as evil or embraced as good by the governing class and its "amen chorus" of nationalist/patriots depending on only one question: Who's doing the deed?

For establishment politicians American exceptionalism is a catechism that must be spoken in order to enter "the spectrum of acceptable opinion": if you're not wearing an American flag pin and asking God to bless America above all others, if you're not genuflecting before the altar of American exceptionalism, you're banished from the arena with no right to speak at all.

The brilliant soliloquy by Will McAvoy (played by Jeff Daniels) on the TV show *Newsroom* shined a necessary light into that darkness. A hard-bitten reporter decides to cut the crap when a college student asks, "Why is America the greatest country in the world?" He points out that the United States is seventh in the world in literacy, forty-ninth in life expectancy, and one hundred seventy-eighth in infant mortality. "We lead the world in only three categories," he asserts: number of incarcerated fellow citizens, military spending, and number of adults who believe in angels. The bit went viral as "America is not the greatest country in the world."

"The American Dream" is the domestic twin of American exceptionalism, and it performs as a kind of social Rorschach test—it could mean a one-family home in the suburbs with a two-car garage to some, marital bliss plus two beautiful and above-average children to others, or a partridge in a pear tree. Maybe it's job security or a career, good health or a pension when you're old, a college education for the kids, or season tickets to the Bulls or the Warriors. Yes, yes, yes—achieving the American Dream includes picking up some or preferably all of the above. But the dream can also include rampant consumerism and unchecked acquisition, the freedom to acquire unlimited cash and shop till you drop. It surely implies mobility and climbing spryly up the social ladder ahead of the less worthy. Every cheery politician or run-of-the-mill billionaire will happily tell anyone who will listen: "I'm living the American Dream." It's a stuttering echo throughout the culture, the irresistible comfort food of all cliches—it may not be healthy, but it feels good going down.

One part sunny fantasy like the green light at the end of Daisy's dock, one part hackneyed chestnut, the American Dream is a contradiction and most often a deadly illusion— less a concrete, shared aspiration than a shadowy, shapeless phantom reminiscent of the corruption, longing, and despair at the hollow heart of Gatsby's delusion. Because if the American Dream can mean absolutely anything, then it also means nothing at all.

Yes, the Statue of Liberty still stands in New York harbor with that raised torch and the well-known message of generosity and hope written by Emma Lazarus: "Give me your tired, your poor, your huddled masses yearning to breathe free, the wretched refuse of your teeming shore. Send these, the homeless, tempest-tossed to me. I lift my lamp beside the golden door!" And yes, that lovely sentiment is undermined daily by our domestic politics, the ugly reality of armed militiamen turning immigrants back at the border, massive detention camps, racial and ethnic and religious profiling, and calls for a national registry for Arabs and Muslims.

Rejecting the suffocating dogma and entangling repercussions of the American Dream is a step toward connecting with our own more authentic human hopes, our community plans and projects, our human-sized dreams and aspirations. If everyone would take a moment to gather in the assembly or the coliseum or the theater, the community center, park, or town square; if we would face one another more authentically, without masks, as who and what we really are, and, importantly, who we aspire to be in the world; if we could speak more directly and plainly to one another and share in just a few words our deepest dreams about how we want to live and where we want to go and what gives meaning to our lives — in that free space and from that wild diversity, a more honest and humane dream could surely emerge: *out of many, one.*

* * *

The revolutionary Martin Luther King Jr. was more than an American dreamer—he was an angry pilgrim who set himself on a righteous journey toward justice. He was still the energetic southern preacher of his earliest days in the movement, still the activist and nonviolent warrior, widening his focus to include economic as well as racial justice, world peace as well as nonviolence. In 1967 he wrote: "For years I labored with the idea of reforming the existing institutions of the society, a little change here, a little change there. Now I feel quite differently. I think you've got to have a reconstruction of the entire society, a revolution of values."[2]

His revolutionary dream was spelled out in sermons, speeches, books, and published writings from 1965 until he was assassinated in 1968. His vision of a better world linked racial equality with economic justice and bound those to the struggle for global justice and peace. In the last years of his life, Reverend King spoke consistently of combating the triple evils of racism, poverty, and war.

The official Martin Luther King Jr. story is a central part of the American myth, taught to schoolchildren and remembered at prayer breakfasts on the national holiday in his name: there was once a bad time in America when some terrible white people mistreated Black people, but then a saint came along with vision that would transfigure us; he had a dream and gave a speech; he led a boycott and then a march; he won a Nobel Prize. Now we all get along fine. Thank you,

Martin Luther King Jr. It's comforting, perhaps, but it rings false on every count.

Reverend King was an activist for only thirteen years of his short life, and the revolutions in his own thinking over that time were breathtaking. By 1965 he was exhausted and fearful, convinced that America could not be changed through protest alone. He had been defeated again and again—in Chicago, in Memphis—and his allies were rapidly abandoning him. When he demanded economic justice, organized the Poor People's Campaign, and came out decisively against the invasion and occupation of Vietnam, most of his establishment associates (who had joined late in any case) turned away. He kept on; he stayed the course. By the time he was murdered on April 4, 1968, his approval rating in opinion polls had sunk below 35 percent.

"Insane generosity," Albert Camus wrote in *The Rebel*, "is the generosity of rebellion." It may be that man is mortal, he said, "but let us die resisting; and if our lot is complete annihilation, let us not behave in such a way that it seems justice!" Camus evoked a generosity that consistently refused unfairness and made no calculation as to what that refusal offered in return. "Real generosity toward the future," Camus concluded, "lies in giving all to the present." Giving it all, here and now, fully animating our moment in the light between those two infinities of darkness. "I can't do everything," we hear a friend lamenting. "Time is short, and I am small." True. But can you do anything—anything at all? Anything is where you begin. King gave it all, a generous warrior for the future—our future.

The revolutionary King is not the one honored at Senate gatherings or congressional prayer meetings, but the man's whole life remains important. The controversy over the King statue in the National Mall is emblematic: reactionary lawmakers complained that the commissioned statue made him look "angry." Yes it did, and yes he was.

The title of his last book was *Where Do We Go from Here: Chaos or Community?*—an excellent question then, and a dramatically more urgent question today. Where do we go from here: chaos or community, socialism or barbarism, the end of capitalism or the end of Earth?

Enter the territory of agitation and organizing and movement building. A glance at history shows us that broad and deep transformations are always the result of mobilized popular movements, and that the exploited and oppressed are the true engines of social progress. Lyndon Johnson passed the most far-reaching civil rights legislation since Reconstruction, but he was never part of the rising Black freedom movement. Franklin Delano Roosevelt led significant legislative advances in workers' rights and social welfare, but he was not part of the powerful labor movement of the time. And Abraham Lincoln, who issued the Emancipation Proclamation ending chattel slavery in the Confederacy, never belonged to an abolitionist party. These three presidents are remembered for Earth-shaking accomplishments, yet none of them acted alone, and in fact each was reacting to intense and sustained fire from below.

Thousands, tens of thousands, and millions right now are mobilizing to stoke those fires from below, to develop a shared faith that injustice can be opposed and justice aspired to, that human solidarity and connectedness can become a living force, that a spirit of outrage can be tempered with vast feelings of love and generosity, and that a full and passionate embrace of the lives we're given can be combined with an eagerness to move forward toward a worldwide beloved community.

We are relentlessly told by the defenders of the status quo that whatever problems we encounter are personal and not social, and that any political problems will only be solved by the elite. Our job is to stare wistfully at the power we have little or no access to: the White House, the medieval auction block called the Congress, the Supreme Court, and more. These can be sites of struggle, to be sure, but if we become mesmerized or caught in their thrall we diminish our own confidence in ourselves and mishandle our own latent collective power, the power we have full access to: in the shop and the factory and the workplace, the neighborhood and the community and the street, the school and the classroom— which for ordinary people is more real and more relevant than the distant power shaped by wealth and theft.

We will not bring a social movement into being through willpower alone, but neither does it make sense to wait patiently for a movement to present itself, springing fully formed from the head of Zeus. The world we need and desire will be forged in action by people struggling for something better, working together in common cause, developing and transforming ourselves as we gather momentum and energy in the hopeful tradition of revolution. We must open our eyes, we must act, and we must rethink and start again. The painstaking work begins, and it can never really be finished.

Part of movement building involves breaking from the "TINA" trap: There Is No Alternative. The privileged and the powerful insist that we accept on faith that this is the best of all possible worlds, and that even with all of its imperfections, it is inevitable and, well, There Is No Alternative. The agitator and organizer, the activist and revolutionary posit alternatives, demonstrate in a thousand ways that the world as such is a choice, and then mobilize to reach for our dreams and demand the impossible.

Working together against war and empire and environmental degradation, struggling shoulder to shoulder for racial and gender justice, labor, and human rights, we search for and find our common interests as we expand our sense of expectation and possibility. Learning to talk and work together is itself a hopeful, rebel act in these difficult and exciting times. Struggles in the streets build cooperation and solidarity as we reject the neoliberal and austerity traps imposed by capital.

That possible other world is a world of socialism with participatory democracy and freedom, a world in which the needs of people come before profit and active participation is constantly mobilized. Explicitly rejecting capitalism is essential for movement-builders today—capitalism has no answers to the crises we face, and zombie capitalism, casino capitalism, Wizard-of-Oz capitalism is in fact the root of the problem. Insisting that the socialist alternative we fight for is inseparably tied to democracy is also indispensable—we must create a space where workers of every type plan, manage, and control in order to satisfy social needs. Authentic democracy mobilizes the capacities of working folks and the broad masses of people to define the society we want and need, embracing the revolutionary practice of simultaneously changing circumstances and changing ourselves.

We reject the logic of the rich and the powerful; we rethink and recast issues in more robust and humane frames; we connect the issues in order to find our natural allies and comrades and to develop a more comprehensive view. Whoever we are and wherever we work and play, we must remind ourselves that movements don't make themselves. It's up to each and all of us to arise every day with our minds set on freedom, and to commit to movement building as a regular and required part of what we do.

On the important issues of the last two centuries, America's radicals from Ida B. Wells Barnett, Jane Addams, and Emma Goldman to John Brown, Harriet Tubman, Eugene Debs, and W. E. B. Du Bois have gotten it right by going to the root of matters. The legacy continued with the work of Ella Baker, Septima Clark, Shulamith Firestone, Gloria Steinem, Dorothy Day to Martin Luther King Jr. and Malcolm X forty years ago and on up to today and the efforts of James

Thindwa, Bill Fletcher, and Karen Lewis, Grace Lee Boggs, Ai-jen Poo, Naomi Klein, Medea Benjamin, Kathy Boudin, Michelle Alexander, Angela Davis, Kathy Kelly, Barbara Ransby, Asha Rosa, and Reyna Wences. Of course, as Ella Baker said of Reverend King, "Martin didn't make the movement, the movement made Martin," and it's true: For every remembered leader there were thousands, tens of thousands, and millions putting their shoulders on history's wheel and sharing a faith that injustice can be opposed and justice aspired to, a belief in human solidarity and connectedness as a living force, a spirit of outrage tempered with vast feelings of love and generosity, a commitment to open-ended dialogue where the questions are always open to debate, and a full and passionate embrace of the life we're given combined with an eagerness to move forward striving to build a worldwide beloved community.

In 1894 Eugene Debs was jailed for six months for violating an injunction against supporting the Pullman Strike, and a hundred thousand people gathered in the rain in Chicago to greet him upon his release. He linked the cause of labor to the aspirations of the revolutionaries of 1776, and famously said, "If I could lead you into the Promised Land, I would not do it, for someone else would come along and lead you out." And in that same year the philosopher John Dewey took a teaching position at the University of Chicago, and wrote to his wife that "Chicago is the place to make you appreciate at every turn the opportunity which chaos affords."[3]

Chaos and opportunity—a constant contradiction in America, always another incongruity or disparity or dispute or deviation to look into, always a challenge, an opposition or an absurdity, and until the end of time another pathway opening. As I noted earlier, standing directly next to the world as such—the world we see and the places we take for granted—stands another world, a possible world, a world that could be or should be, but is not yet. And that's surely a good thing because *contradiction may save us*. Nothing is settled, once and for all, everything is on the move and in the mix, and there's much more to know, and to do. We're in the middle of the muddle—right from the start.

In our pursuit of a world powered by love and reaching toward joy and justice, imagination is our most formidable and unyielding ally—the people's common asset, an endowment to each one and the indispensable weapon of the powerless. Yes, they control the massive military-industrial complex, the sophisticated surveillance systems, the prison cells, and the organized propaganda—and these are on constant display as if to remind us every minute that there is no hope of a world without the instruments of death and oppression—and we have only our minds, our desires, and our dreams—and each other. And, yes, in a fixed war or a traditional conflict we are finished before we start. But it's also true that there's no power on Earth stronger than the imagination unleashed and the collective human soul on fire. In irregular combat or a guerrilla struggle that pits our free imaginations against the stillborn and stunted imaginations of the war-makers and the mercenaries, we will win.

When we choose life, we leap into the whirlwind with courage and hope. Hope is a choice, after all, and confidence a politics—our collective antidote to cynicism and despair. It's the capacity to notice or invent alternatives, and then to do something about it, to get busy in projects of repair. I have a T-shirt that reads: "Depressed? Maybe it's political."

The future is entirely unknown and unknowable; optimism, then, is simply idle dreaming, while pessimism is no more than a dreary turn of mind—they are twins, two sides of the same deterministic coin. Both optimists and pessimists delude themselves into thinking they know for sure what's coming. They don't; no one does. The day before Rosa Parks sat down on that bus, Jim Crow was immutable; the day after, the Third American Revolution was unstoppable. The day before John Brown's assault on Harpers Ferry, the end of slavery was impossible; the day after, abolition was inevitable. The day before the Zapatistas declared a state of war against Mexico from its small base in Chiapas, the idea of a peasant and indigenous-led civil resistance was unthinkable; now it is a model for actions across the globe. And had I been asked my advice on the day before Occupy Wall Street set up those tents, I'd have said it won't be effective; the day after, I dived in headfirst.

Choosing hopefulness is holding out the *possibility* of change. It's living with one foot in the mud and muck of the world as it is, while another foot strides forward toward a world that could be. Hope is never a matter of sitting down and waiting patiently; hope is nourished in action, and it assumes that we are—each and all of us—incomplete as human beings. We have things to do, mountains to climb, problems to solve, injuries to heal. We can *choose* to see life as infused with the capacity to cherish happiness, to respect evidence and argument and reason, to uphold integrity, and to imagine a world more loving, more peaceful, more joyous, and more just than the one we were given—and we should. Of course we live in dark times, and some of us inhabit even darker places, and, yes, we act mostly in the dark. But we are never freer as teachers and students, citizens, residents, activists and organizers, and artists and thinkers than when we shake ourselves free and refuse to see the situation or the world before us as the absolute end of the matter.

The planet is as it is—a mass of contradictions and tragedies; rich with beauty and human accomplishment, vicious with human denial; an organism that drains us and replenishes us at the same time, gives us life and kills us—and it's asking us to dive in: study, imagine, ask queer questions, read, learn, organize, talk to strangers, mobilize, and display our ethical aspirations publicly. We might take a page from that great poet/teacher Walt Whitman:

> Love the earth and sun and the animals, despise riches, give alms to everyone that asks, stand up for the stupid and crazy, devote your income and labor to others, hate tyrants, argue not concerning God, have patience and indulgence toward the people, take off your hat to nothing known or unknown or to any man or number for men, go freely with powerful uneducated persons and with the young and with the mothers of families, re-examine all you have been told at school or church or in any book, dismiss whatever insults your own soul.[4]

Turn out all the lights and ignite a small candle in any corner of the room. That little light held aloft anywhere challenges the darkness everywhere. One candle. We can always do something, and something is where we begin. The tools are everywhere—humor and art, protest and spectacle, the quiet, patient intervention and the angry and urgent thrust—and the rhythm of and recipe for activism is always the same: We open our eyes and look unblinkingly at the immense and dynamic world we find before us; we allow ourselves to be astonished by the beauty and horrified at the suffering all around us; we organize ourselves, link hands with others, dive in, speak up, and act out; we doubt that our efforts have made the important difference we'd hoped for, and so we rethink, recalibrate, look again, and dive in once more.

The great rebel Rosa Luxemburg, jailed for her opposition to World War I, lived her life to that rhythm. She sent a letter from prison to a friend and comrade who'd complained to her that their revolutionary work was suffering terribly without Luxemburg's day-to-day leadership. First, Red Rosa wrote, stop whining—excellent advice in any circumstance. She went on to urge her friend to be more of a mensch. Oh, I can't define mensch for you, she said, but what I mean is that you should strive to be a person who loves your own life enough to appreciate the sunset and the sunrise, to enjoy a bottle of wine over dinner with friends, or to take a walk by the sea. But you must also love the world enough to put your shoulder on history's great wheel when history demands it. Working that out may become for each and all of us a collective daily challenge—it's also the way forward toward commitment and balance.

Choose life; choose possibility; choose rebellion and revolution. Be a mensch.

Demand the impossible!

ACKNOWLEDGMENTS

Thanks to the comrades at Haymarket Books: Julie Fain for her encouragement and wise interventions from the start, Jason Farbman, Rory Fanning, and Jim Plank for their dedicated efforts, Ruth Baldwin for super-smart editing early on, Anthony Arnove for his confidence in this project, and the remarkable Dao X. Tran, for whom every word matters. And thanks to Boyd Bellinger for his brilliant research assistance. Everlasting thanks to Nathaly Bonilla—sister, comrade, friend, and artist of the better angels.

APPENDIX
INDEXES AND SOURCES

Military-Industrial Complex Index

1. Year the United States established what
would become a standing army: 1940

2. Rank of United States in military spending worldwide: 1

3. Percent of world's total military budget: 34

4. Percent increase in US military spending between
1998 and 2011 (in constant 2011 dollars): 88

5. Total US military spending annually (in 2014): $609,914,000,000

6. Minimum number of US military bases in foreign countries: 587

7. Number of foreign military installations based on US territory: 0

8. Amount of money to private defense
corporations in FY 2015: $272,790,578,374

9. Percent to top five contractors in 2015: 27

10. Rank of United States as a global arms dealer (2015): 1

1. Selective Training and Service Act of 1940, Pub. L. 76–783, 54 Stat. 885.
2. Sam Perlo-Freeman, Aude Fleurant, Pieter D. Wezeman, and
Siemon T. Wezeman, "Trends in World Military Expenditure,
2014," Stockholm International Peace Research Institute, April 2015,
http://books.sipri.org/files/FS/SIPRIFS1504.pdf.
3. Ibid.

4. Stockholm International Peace Research Institute, SIPRI Military Expenditure Database [data file], 2015. Retrieved from www.sipri .org/research/armaments/milex/milex_database/milex_database.

5. Ibid.

6. United States Department of Defense, *Base Structure Report: Fiscal Year 2015 Baseline*, n.d., www.acq.osd.mil/eie/Downloads /Reports/Base%20Structure%20Report%20FY15.pdf.

8. United States Government, Department of Defense, Contract Data [data file], 2015. Retrieved from www.usaspending.gov/Transparency/ Pages/AgencyContracts.aspx?AgencyCode=9700&FiscalYear=2015.

9. Ibid.

10. Stockholm International Peace Research Institute, SIPRI Arms Transfers Database [data file], 2016. Retrieved from www.sipri.org /databases/armstransfers/armstransfers.

Prison Complex Index

1. Change in the rate of incarceration in the past forty years (1972–2012): +439%

2. Rank of a metaphorical "Correctional Supervision City" by population for all US cities (2014): 2

3. Rank of the US incarcerated population in the world (most recent figures for all countries): 1

4. Percent of all of the world's prisoners in US prisons (most recent figures for all countries): 21

5. Percent of Americans engaged in "guard labor"— defending property, supervising work, or otherwise keeping their fellow Americans in line (2002): 26.1

6. Rate of juveniles detained in the United States to all comparison nations combined (US figures from 2006): 5.5:1

7. Average annual cost to keep a juvenile in detention in the United States in 2011: $148,767

8. Average annual cost per child to fund
US schools, 2010–2011: $12,926

9. Year that the US Supreme Court ruled that solitary
confinement caused prisoners to fall into "a semi-fatuous
condition, from which it was next to impossible to arouse
them, and others became violently insane": 1890

10. Estimated number of inmates in solitary
confinement in "supermax" prisons (2005): 25,000

1. Jeremy Travis, Bruce Western, and Steve Reburn, eds., *The Growth of Incarceration in the United States: Exploring Causes and Consequences* (Washington, DC: National Academies Press, 2014).
2. Danielle Kaeble, Lauren Glaze, Anastasios Tsoutis, and Todd Minton, *Correctional Populations in the United States, 2014*, revised January 2016 (Bureau of Justice Statistics, U.S. Department of Justice), www.bjs.gov/content/pub/pdf/cpus14.pdf.
3. International Centre for Prison Studies, *Highest to Lowest: Prison Population Total* [data file] (n.d.), World Prison Brief, Institute for Criminal Policy Research, www.prisonstudies.org/highest -to-lowest/prison-population-total?field_region_taxonomy_tid=All.
4. Ibid.
5. S. Bowles and A. Jayadev, "Garrison America," *Economists' Voice* 4, no. 2 (2007): 1–7.
6. "Factsheet: Juvenile Justice," *Finding Direction: Expanding Criminal Justice Options by Considering Policies of Other Nations*, Justice Policy Institute, April 2011, www.justicepolicy.org/uploads/justicepolicy/documents/juvenile_justice.pdf.
7. *Sticker Shock: Calculating the Full Price Tag for Youth Incarceration*, Justice Policy Institute, December 2014, www.justicepolicy.org/uploads/justicepolicy/documents/executive_summary_-_sticker_shock_final.pdf.
8. "Digest of Education Statistics: Total and Current Expenditures per Pupil in Public Elementary and Secondary Schools: Selected Years, 1919–20 through 2012–13" [data file], National Center for Education Statistics, 2015, http://nces.ed.gov/programs/digest/d15/tables/dt15_236.55.asp
9. In re Medley, 134 U.S. 160, 161 (U.S. 1890).

10. Daniel P. Mears, Evaluating the Effectiveness of Supermax Prisons, January 2006, www.ncjrs.gov/pdffiles1/nij/grants/211971.pdf.

Economic Complex Index

1. Percent of Swedish workers in trade unions (2013): 67.7

2. Percent of US workers in trade unions (2013): 10.8

3. Percent of unionized private-sector US workers in 1900/2015: 6.7/6.7

4. Hours American workers work (as a percentage) compared to their UK, Norwegian, and Dutch counterparts (2013): + 7, +27, +30

5. Rank of US in terms of income per hour worked in manufacturing (2010): 11

6. Number of countries whose GDP is less than the combined fortunes of the five wealthiest Americans (2013): At least 149

7. Ratio of net worth of the wealthiest 400 Americans to the 150 million poorest Americans (2009): 1/1

8. Percent change in Wall Street profits from 2007 to 2009: +720

9. Percent change in unemployment rate from 2007 to 2009: +102

10. Percent change in total home equity from 2006 to 2009: –61

1. *Trade Union Density* [data set], Organisation for Economic Co-operation and Development (n.d.), http://stats.oecd.org/Index.aspx DataSetCode=UN_DEN.
2. Ibid.
3. "Union Members Summary," Economic New Release, Bureau of Labor Statistics, U.S. Department of Labor, January 28, 2016, www.bls.gov/news.release/union2.nr0.htm.
4. *Average Annual Hours Actually Worked per Worker* [data set], Organisation for Economic Co-operation and Development (n.d.), http://stats.oecd.org/index.aspx?DataSetCode=ANHRS.

5. *Global Wage Report 2012/2013: Wages and Equitable Growth* (Geneva: International Labour Organization, 2013), www.ilo.org /wcmsp5/groups/public/—dgreports/—dcomm/—publ/documents /publication/wcms_194843.pdf.
6. Luisa Kroll, "Inside the 2013 Forbes 400: Facts and Figures on America's Richest," *Forbes*, September 16, 2013, www.forbes.com /sites/luisakroll/2013/09/16/inside-the-2013-forbes-400-facts-and -figures-on-americas-richest/#18fe6a1b3af5; *Gross Domestic Product 2013*, World Bank (n.d.), http://databank.worldbank.org/data /download/GDP.pdf.
7. Tom Kertscher, "Michael Moore Says 400 Americans Have More Wealth Than Half of All Americans Combined," *PolitiFact Wisconsin*, 2011, www.politifact.com/wisconsin/statements/2011/mar/10/michael -moore/michael-moore-says-400-americans-have-more-wealth-/.
8. *The Securities Industry in New York City*, Office of the State Comptroller, November 2010, http://osc.state.ny.us/osdc/rpt10-2011.pdf.
9. *Annual Average Unemployment Rate, Civilian Labor Force 16 Years and Over (percent)* [data set], Labor Force Statistics from the Current Population Survey, Bureau of Labor Statistics, n.d., www.bls.gov/cps/ prev_yrs.htm.
10. Rajashri Chakrabarti et al., *Household Debt and Saving during the 2007 Recession*, Federal Reserve Bank of New York, January 2011, www.newyorkfed.org/medialibrary/media/research/staff_reports/ sr482.pdf.

Debt Index

1. Average amount of student loan debt for all graduating seniors with student loans (2014): $28,950

2. Average amount of student loan debt for all graduating seniors with student loans (1994): $10,100

3. Total outstanding student loan debt (May 2013): $1.2 trillion

4. Household net worth lost during Great Recession: $16.4 trillion

5. Percentage of inflation-adjusted median wealth lost by African American households (2005–2009): 66

6. Ratio of white/African American median household net worth, 2005 vs. 2010: 12/1 vs. 22/1

7. Foreclosure starts (2008–2012): 8,659,644

8. US credit card debt (January 2016): $935.3 billion

9. Developing countries' total external debt in current US dollars (2014): $5,393,390,684,030.80

1. "Student Debt and the Class of 2014," press release, Institute for College Access & Success, October 27, 2015, http://ticas.org/sites/default/files/pub_files/student_debt_and_the_class_of_2014_nr_0.pdf.

2. "Trends in Debt for Bachelor's Degree Recipients a Year after Graduation: 1994, 2001, and 2009," web tables, U.S. Department of Education, December 2012, http://nces.ed.gov/pubs2013/2013156.pdf.

3. Rohit Chopra, *Student Debt Swells, Federal Loans Now Top a Trillion*, Consumer Finance Protection Bureau, July 17, 2013, www.consumerfinance.gov/newsroom/student-debt-swells-federal-loans-now-top-a-trillion/.

4. Chris Isidore, "America's Lost Trillions," CNN Money, June 9, 2011, http://money.cnn.com/2011/06/09/news/economy/household_wealth/.

5. Rakesh Kochhar, Richard Fry, and Paul Taylor, "Wealth Gaps Rise to Record Highs between Whites, Blacks, Hispanics," Pew Research Center, July 26, 2011, www.pewsocialtrends.org/2011/07/26/wealth-gaps-rise-to-record-highs-between-whites-blacks-hispanics.

6. Tami Luhby, "Worsening Wealth Inequality by Race," *CNN Money*, June 21, 2012, http://money.cnn.com/2012/06/21/news/economy/wealth-gap-race.

7. Joanne W. Hsu, David A. Matsa, and Brian Melzer, "Positive Externalities of Social Insurance: Unemployment Insurance and Consumer Credit," July 15, 2014, http://dx.doi.org/10.2139/ssrn.2185198.

8. *Consumer Credit* [data file], Board of Governors of the Federal Reserve System, March 2016, www.federalreserve.gov/releases/g19/current.

9. "World DataBank: International Debt Statistics" [data file], World Bank (n.d.) http://databank.worldbank.org/data/reports.aspx?source=international-debt-statistics.

Cops Index

1. Amount of military equipment transferred to local police forces, 1997–2014: more than $4.3 billion

2. Paid to citizens because of police violence or misbehavior in five years (2010–2014) in New York: $601 million
   3. Chicago: $250 million
   4. Los Angeles: $57 million
   5. Philadelphia: $54 million
   6. Baltimore: $12 million

7. Percentage of city budget dedicated to police in Baltimore (2011–2012): 20

8. Percentage of city budget dedicated to police in Oakland: 40

9. Number of civilian complaints concerning police misconduct in Chicago between March 2011 and September 2015: 28,567

10. Percentage of complaints that resulted in a police officer receiving discipline: less than 2

1. Zoë Carpenter, "Will Congress Finally Put a Dent in the $4.3 Billion in Surplus Military Equipment Going to Police Departments?" *Congress* (blog), *Nation*, September 8, 2014, www.thenation.com /article/one-month-after-michael-browns-shooting-lawmakers -examine-police-militarization.

2. Zusha Elinson and Dan Frosch, "Cost of Police-Misconduct Cases Soars in Big U.S. Cities: Data Show Rising Payouts for Police-Misconduct Settlements and Court Judgments," *Wall Street Journal*, July 15, 2015, www.wsj.com/articles/cost-of-police-misconduct-cases-soars-in-big-u-s-cities-1437013834.

3. Darwin BondGraham, "Throwing More Money at Police," *East Bay Express*, May 29, 2013, www.eastbayexpress.com/oakland/throwing-more-money-at-police/Content?oid=3560590; *Budget 2012 Overview* (Chicago: City of Chicago, 2011), www.cityofchicago.org/dam/city/ depts/obm/supp_info/2012%20Budget/2012BudgetOverview.pdf.

4. BondGraham, "Throwing More Money."

5. Ibid.
6. Ibid.
7. Ibid.
8. Ibid.
9. *Citizens Police Data Project* [data set], Invisible Institute, n.d., https://cpdb.co/data/DqJV3L/citizens-police-data-project.
10. Ibid.

Health Care Index

1. Rank of United States among eleven wealthy countries in health system performance (2013): 11

2. Rank of United States among the countries of the world in annual per capita public and private health care spending (2013): 3

3. Life expectancy in years of a typical US citizen (2012): 79

4. Rank of United States out of 224 countries in average life expectancy (2015): 43

5. Administrative costs as a percent of hospital spending in the United States/Canada (2011): 25.32/12.42

6. Number of Black/white deaths per 1000 in the first month of life (2013): 7.46/3.34

7. Number of Black/white deaths per 1000 in the first year of life (2013): 11.11/5.06

8. Number of Black/white children under age two who contract bacterial meningitis per 100,000 (2005): 26/11

9. Cost of Prevnar, a vaccine that prevents diseases (ear infections, pneumonia) caused by pneumococcal bacteria per dose (2014): $136

10. Amount of revenue that Pfizer, the monopolist and sole manufacturer, realized from Prevnar in 2013: $4 billion

1. "Mirror, Mirror on the Wall, 2014 Update: How the U.S. Health Care System Compares Internationally," The Commonwealth Fund, 2014, www.commonwealthfund.org/publications/fund-reports/2014/jun/mirror-mirror.

2. *Health Expenditure per Capita* (current US$) [data file], The World Bank, n.d., http://data.worldbank.org/indicator/SH.XPD.PCAP/countries/1W?order=wbapi_data_value_2013%20wbapi_data_value%20wbapi_data_value-last&sort=desc&display=default.

3. *Life Expectancy Data by Country* [data file], World Health Organization, n.d., http://apps.who.int/gho/data/node.main.3?lang=en.

4. *Life Expectancy Data by World Bank Income Group* [data file], World Health Organization, n.d., http://apps.who.int/gho/data/view.main.700?lang=en.

5. D. U. Himmelstein et al., "A Comparison of Hospital Administrative Costs in Eight Nations: U.S. Costs Exceed All Others by Far," *Health Affairs* 33 (2014): 1586–1594.

6. T. J. Mathews, M. F. MacDorman, and M. E. Thoma, "Infant Mortality Statistics from the 2013 Period, Linked Birth/Infant Death Data Set," *National Vital Statistics* Reports 64, no. 9 (August 6, 2015), www.cdc.gov/nchs/data/nvsr/nvsr64/nvsr64_09.pdf.

7. Ibid.

8. Richard Rothstein and Tamara Wilder, "The Contribution of Black-White Health Differences to the Academic Achievement Gap," *Poverty & Race* (September–October 2005), www.prrac.org/full_text.php?text_id=1050&item_id=9648&newsletter_id=83&header=Health&kc=1.

9. Elizabeth Rosenthal, "The Price of Prevention: Vaccine Costs Are Soaring," *New York Times*, July 2, 2014, www.nytimes.com/2014/07/03/health/Vaccine-Costs-Soaring-Paying-Till-It-Hurts.html.

10. Ibid.

Education Complex Index

1. Annual per pupil budget allocation in District of Columbia Public Schools (2015–2016 academic year): $11,965

2. Annual tuition per student at Sidwell Friends School in Washington, DC (2015–2016): $37,750

3. Arts credits required to graduate from
Sidwell Friends School (2014–2015): 2

4. Arts credits required to graduate from District of
Columbia Public Schools (2014–2015): 0.5

5. Student-to-teacher ratio at Sidwell
Friends School (2013–2014) 7.8:1

6. Student-to-teacher ratio in Washington,
DC schools (2013–2014): 13.32:1

7. Student-to-library-staff (professional and paraprofessional)
ratio at Sidwell Friends School (2014–2015): 191.7:1

8. Student-to-library-staff (professional and paraprofessional)
ratio in District of Columbia Public Schools (2013–2014): 710:1

1. *FY16 School Budget Data* [data file], District of Columbia Public
    Schools, 2015, www.dcpsdatacenter.com/budget_process.html#data.
2. "Tuition and Fees," Sidwell Friends School, www.sidwell.edu
    /admissions/tuition-and-fees/index.aspx.
3. "Upper School Curriculum Guide," Sidwell Friends School, 2014,
    www.sidwell.edu/documents/Curriculum%20Guide_14-15_FINAL.
    pdf.
4. "Graduation Requirements," District of Columbia Public Schools,
    n.d., http://dcps.dc.gov/graduation.
5. *PSS: Private School Universe Survey* [data file], National Center for
    Education Statistics, n.d., https://nces.ed.gov/surveys/pss
    /privateschoolsearch/school_detail.asp?Search=1&SchoolName
    =sidwell+friends&NumOfStudentsRange=more&IncGrade
    =-1&LoGrade=-1&HiGrade=-1&ID=02032143.
6. "Local Education Agency (School District) Universe Survey," U.S.
    Department of Education, National Center for Education Statistics,
    Common Core of Data (CCD), 2013–14, v.1a.
7. "About SFS," Sidwell Friends School, n.d., www.sidwell.edu/about
    _sfs/index.aspx; and "Faculty/Staff Directory," Sidwell Friends
    School, n.d., www.sidwell.edu/directories/index.aspx?FirstName
    =&LastName=&DepartmentTypeID=122&DivisionID=&sortBy
    =LastName&LinkID=&DirectoryModuleID=341&pageaction

=VPFaculty.

8. "District Directory Information: District of Columbia Public Schools," National Center for Education Statistics, n.d., http://nces. ed.gov/ccd/districtsearch/district_detail.asp?Search=1& InstName=district+of+columbia&State=11&DistrictType=1& DistrictType=2&DistrictType=3&DistrictType=4&DistrictType= 5&DistrictType=6&DistrictType=7&NumOfStudentsRange=more& NumOfSchoolsRange=more&ID2=1100030&details=.

Earth Index

1. Monsanto Corporation's annual budget lobbying the US government (2015): $4.3 million

2. Year the FDA approved Monsanto's bovine growth hormone (rBGH)—banned in 31 countries—for use in US cattle: 1993

3. Profits made in the decade from 2001 to 2010 by the top five oil companies: $901.6 billion

4. Profits ExxonMobil averaged each quarter in 2012: $11.225 billion

5. Percent of combined $100 billion 2008 profits the big five devoted to "renewable and alternative energy ventures": 4

6. Percent rise in water utility rates for average Detroit resident in 2015–2016: 9.3

7. Estimated number of Detroit residents affected by water disconnections (as of July 2014): 100,000

8. Value of the Detroit Water and Sewerage Department: $6.4 billion

9. Percent of the DWSD budget that goes to Wall Street banks as debt-service (FY 2016): 45

10. Amount contracted to Homrich, a private contractor hired to disconnect water from Detroiters whose overdue bills exceed $150: up to $5.6 million

1. *Monsanto Co* [data file], OpenSecrets.org, n.d., www.opensecrets .org/lobby/clientsum.php?id=D000000055&year=2015.
2. "Report on Food and Drug Administration's Review of the Safety of Recombinant Bovine Somatotropin," Food and Drug Administration, 2014, www.fda.gov/AnimalVeterinary/SafetyHealth /ProductSafetyInformation/ucm130321.htm.
3. Daniel J. Weiss, "Big Oil's Lust for Tax Loopholes: Oil Prices and Profits Rise While Big Oil Defends Its Tax Loopholes," January 31, 2011, www.americanprogress.org/issues/green/news/2011/01/31 /8951/big-oils-lust-for-tax-loopholes.
4. Chris Isidore, "Exxon Mobil Profit Is Just Short of Record," *CNN Money*, February 1, 2013, http://money.cnn.com/2013/02/01 /news/companies/exxon-mobil-profit/index.html?iid=HP_LN.
5. Daniel J. Weiss and Alexandra Kougentakis, "Big Oil Misers," March 31, 2009, www.americanprogress.org/issues/green/news /2009/03/31/5736/big-oil-misers.
6. Charles E. Ramirez, "Detroit Water Board OKs 2015–16 Rate Hikes," *Detroit News*, March 11, 2015, www.detroitnews.com /story/news/local/wayne-county/2015/03/11/detroit-water-sewer -rate-increases/70166240.
7. Rose Hackman, "What Happens When Detroit Shuts Off the Water of 100,000 People," *Atlantic*, July 17, 2014, www.theatlantic .com/business/archive/2014/07/what-happens-when-detroit-shuts -off-the-water-of-100000-people/374548.
8. "Mapping Project Presentation," Detroiters Resisting Emergency Management, 2016, www.d-rem.org/wp-content/uploads/2016/01 /Mapping-Project-Presentation.pdf.
9. "Meeting Agenda: Finance Committee Meeting," Detroit Water and Sewerage Department, October 12, 2015, www.dwsd.org /downloads_n/about_dwsd/financials/Finance_Committee_Binder _10-12-2015.pdf.
10. "Meeting Agenda," Detroit Water and Sewerage Department, April 24, 2013, www.dwsd.org/downloads_n/about_dwsd/bowc/board_ meetings/2013_final_agendas/bowc_final_agenda_2013-04-24.pdf.

NOTES

Chapter One: Disarm

1. Quoted in Walter L. Hixson, *The Myth of American Diplomacy: National Identity and U.S. Foreign Policy* (New Haven, CT: Yale University Press, 2008), 131.
2. Umberto Eco, "Not Such Wicked Leaks," *voxeurop*, December 2, 2010, www.voxeurop.eu/en/content/article/414871-not-such-wicked-leaks.
3. Smedley D. Butler, *War Is a Racket* (New York: Round Table Press, 1935).
4. Dwight D. Eisenhower, Public Papers of the Presidents (1960), 1035–1040, http://coursesa.matrix.msu.edu/~hst306/documents/indust.html.

Chapter Three: Shoulders to the Wheel

1. E. M. Schumacher, *Small Is Beautiful: A Study of Economics as if People Mattered* (New York: HarperCollins, 2010).
2. James K. Galbraith, "Actually, the Retirement Age Is Too High," *Common Dreams* (originally published in *Foreign Policy*, January 19, 2011), www.commondreams.org/views/2011/01/19/actually-retirement-age-too-high.

Chapter Four: Jubilee

1. Adam Smith, *An Inquiry into the Nature and Causes of the Wealth of Nations* (New York: Modern Library, 1994).
2. Dave Zirin, "How Sports Attack Public Education," Edge of Sports, n.d., www.edgeofsports.com/2010-03-04-507/index. html.

Chapter Five: Stop the Cops

1. Quoted in "A Staggering Moment for Chicago," *Chicago Tribune*, editorial, November 24, 2015, www.chicagotribune. com/news/ct-laquan-video-edit-1125-20151124-story.html.
2. Jamie Kalven, "Sixteen Shots," *Slate*, February 10, 2015, www.slate.com/articles/news_and_politics/politics/2015/02/ laquan_mcdonald_shooting_a_recently_obtained_autopsy _report_on_the_dead.html.
3. "Chicago's Call for Peace over Laquan McDonald Video Does Not Extend to Police Department," Charlene Carruthers interview by Amy Goodman, *Democracy Now*, November 24, 2015, www.truth-out.org/news/item/33780-chicago-s-call-for-peace-over-laquan-mcdonald-video-does-not-extend-to-police-department.
4. Andrew Schroedter, "Chicago Police Misconduct—A Rising Financial Toll," *Public Eye*, Newsletter of Better Government Association, January 31, 2016, www.bettergov.org/news/ chicago-police-misconduct-%E2%80%93-a-rising-finan-cial-toll; *Citizens Police Data Project* [data set], Invisible Institute, n.d., https://cpdb.co/data/D8ygpL/citizens-police -data-project; Andrew Schroedter, "Fatal Shootings by Chicago Police: Tops among Biggest U.S. Cities," July 26, 2015, Better Government Association, www.bettergov.org/news/ fatal-shootings-by-chicago-police-tops-among-biggest-us-cities.
5. Bertolt Brecht, *The Jewish Wife and Other Short Plays*, Eric Bentley, trans. (New York: Grove Press, 1994).
6. Ryan J. Reilly, "FBI Director James Comey Still Unsure If White Supremacist's Attack in Charleston Was Terrorism,"

Huffington Post, July 10, 2015, www.huffingtonpost.
com/2015/07/09/james-comey-charleston-terrorism-_
n_7764614.html.

7. Michael S. Schmidt and Matt Apuzoo, "F.B.I. Chief Links
    Scrutiny of Police with Rise in Violent Crime," *New York
    Times*, October 23, 2015, www.nytimes.com/2015/10/24/us/
    politics/fbi-chief-links-scrutiny-of-police-with-rise-in-violent-
    crime.html.

8. "The Counted," *Guardian*, www.theguardian.com/us-news/
    series/counted-us-police-killings.

Chapter Six: Health Care for All

1. Katherine Eban, "OxyContin: Purdue Pharma's Painful Med-
    icine," *Fortune*, November 9, 2011, http://fortune.com
    /2011/11/09/oxycontin-purdue-pharmas-painful-medicine/.

2. "More U.S. Children Being Diagnosed with Youthful Tendency
    Disorder," *Onion*, September 27, 2000, www.theonion.com
    /article/more-us-children-being-diagnosed-with-youthful-ten-248.

3. *Poverty & Race*, 14, no. 5 (2005): 3.

4. Dr. Martin Luther King Jr., March 25, 1966, 2nd National
    Convention of the Medical Committee for Human Rights,
    quoted on "Health Disparities" page of the Washington State
    Commission of African American Affairs website, www.caa.
    wa.gov/priorities/health/HealthDisparities.shtml.

5. Alex Morris, "The War on Planned Parenthood," *Rolling
    Stone*, April 21, 2016, 60.

6. Julie Creswell, "Race Is On to Profit from Rise of Urgent
    Care," *New York Times*, July 9, 2014, www.nytimes.com/
    2014/07/10/business/race-is-on-to-profit-from-rise-of-urgent-
    care.html.

7. Ibid.

8. Elisabeth Rosenthal, "The Price of Prevention: Vaccine Costs
    Are Soaring," *New York Times*, July 2, 2014, www.nytimes.
    com/2014/07/03/health/Vaccine-Costs-Soaring-Paying-Till-It
    -Hurts.html.

9. See "Tea Party Debate, Part 1," YouTube video, posted by DakotaVoice, September 12, 2011, www.youtube.com/watch?v =yu0HTlxWjHI.

Chapter Seven: Teach Freedom

1. Charles Cobb, "Prospectus for a Freedom School Program (1963)," in *Radical Teacher* 40 (1991): 36.
2. Paulo Freire, *Pedagogy of the Oppressed* (New York: Continuum, 1985), 67.
3. See "Nice White Lady," MAD-TV, YouTube video, posted by Klaustrophobic, July 12, 2007, www.youtube.com/watch?v =ZVF-nirSq5s.
4. Quoted in Cheryl Clark, *"After Mecca": Women Poets and the Black Arts Movement* (New Brunswick, NJ: Rutgers University Press, 2004), 28.

Chapter Eight: Love the Earth

1. Rebecca Solnit, "Power in Paris," *Harper's Magazine*, December 2015, http://harpers.org/archive/2015/12/power-in-paris.

Beginning Again

1. Quoted in Micha Zeko, "The Myth of the Indispensable Nation," *Foreign Policy*, November 6, 2016, http://foreignpolicy. com/2014/11/06/the-myth-of-the-indispensable-nation/.
2. Quoted in Michael Eric Dyson, "No Small Dreams," special to *Britannica.com*, January 17, 2000, www.hartford-hwp.com /archives/45a/288.html.
3. Quoted in Kenan Heise, "Why in Chicago?," *Chicago Daily Defender*, July 9, 2008.
4. Quoted in Garrison Keillor, "The Writer's Almanac," National Public Radio, July 4, 2011.

INDEX

"Passim" (literally "scattered") indicates intermittent discussion of a topic over a cluster of pages.

About Haymarket

Haymarket Books is a nonprofit, progressive book distributor and publisher, a project of the Center for Economic Research and Social Change. We believe that activists need to take ideas, history, and politics into the many struggles for social justice today. Learning the lessons of past victories, as well as defeats, can arm a new generation of fighters for a better world. As Karl Marx said, "The philosophers have merely interpreted the world; the point however is to change it."

We take inspiration and courage from our namesakes, the Haymarket Martyrs, who gave their lives fighting for a better world. Their 1886 struggle for the eight-hour day, which gave us May Day, the international workers' holiday, reminds workers around the world that ordinary people can organize and struggle for their own liberation. These struggles continue today across the globe—struggles against oppression, exploitation, hunger, and poverty.

It was August Spies, one of the Martyrs who was targeted for being an immigrant and an anarchist, who predicted the battles being fought to this day. "If you think that by hanging us you can stamp out the labor movement," Spies told the judge, "then hang us. Here you will tread upon a spark, but here, and there, and behind you, and in front of you, and everywhere, the flames will blaze up. It is a subterranean fire. You cannot put it out. The ground is on fire upon which you stand."

We could not succeed in our publishing efforts without the generous financial support of our readers. Many people contribute to our project through the Haymarket Sustainers program, where donors receive free books in return for their monetary support. If you would like to be a part of this program, please contact us at info@haymarketbooks.org.

Also Available from Haymarket Books

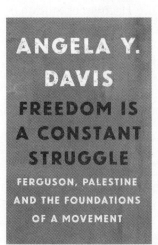

Freedom Is a Constant Struggle: Ferguson, Palestine, and the Foundations of a Movement
Angela Y. Davis
In these newly collected essays, interviews, and speeches, world-renowned activist and scholar Angela Y. Davis illuminates the connections between struggles against state violence and oppression throughout history and around the world.

From #BlackLivesMatter to Black Liberation
Keeanga-Yamahtta Taylor
In this stirring and insightful analysis, activist and scholar Keeanga-Yamahtta Taylor surveys the historical and contemporary ravages of racism and persistence of structural inequality such as mass incarceration and Black unemployment. In this context, she argues that this new struggle against police violence holds the potential to reignite a broader push for Black liberation.

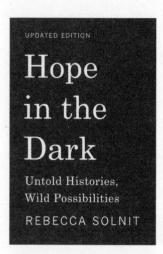

Hope in the Dark: Untold Histories, Wild Possibilities
Updated Edition
Rebecca Solnit
Originally published in 2004, now with a new foreword and afterword, Solnit's influential book shines a light into the darkness of our time in an unforgettable new edition.

Socialism . . . Seriously: A Brief Guide to Human Liberation
Danny Katch
Socialism...Seriously brings together the two great Marxist traditions of Karl and Groucho to provide an entertaining and insightful introduction to what the socialist tradition has to say about democracy, economics, and the potential of human beings to be something more than being bomb-dropping, planet-destroying racist fools.

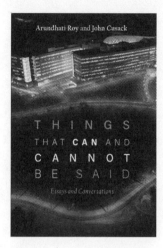

Things That Can and Cannot Be Said
Arundhati Roy and John Cusack

In these provocative and penetrating discussions, Roy and Cusack discuss the nature of the state, empire, and surveillance in an era of perpetual war, the meaning of flags and patriotism, the role of foundations and NGOs in limiting dissent, and the ways in which capital but not people can freely cross borders.